A Picture Postcard History
of

Baseball

by Ron Menchine

Introduction by Ernie Harwell

ALMAR PRESS
BOOK PUBLISHERS

4105 Marietta Drive, Vestal NY 13850
(607) 722-0265 and 6251

14.95

DEDICATION

I dedicate this book to my late father, Judge W. Albert Menchine who first introduced me to Baseball, and to the late Merrell M. Whittlesey, who was a close friend and well-known Washington sportswriter.

Library of Congress Cataloging-in-Publication Data

Menchine, Ron, 1934-
A Picture Postcard History of Baseball / by Ron Menchine:
introduction by Ernie Harwell
    p. cm.
Includes bibliograpical references (p.) and index
ISBN 0-930256-21-2
1. Baseball—United States—History. 2. Postcards—United States —History. I. Title. II
Title: Baseball
GV863.A1M46 1993
796.357'0973—dc20

                  92-16270
                  CIP

Copyright © 1992 by Ron Menchine
                P.O. Box 1
                Long Green, Maryland 21092

First Edition, First Printing......November 1992

PRINTED IN THE UNITED STATES OF AMERICA

Published by: ALMAR PRESS
                4105 Marietta Drive
                Vestal, New York 13850

For a complete catalog of "A Picture Postcard History" Books covering many subjects and a variety of other publications contact the ALMAR PRESS, 4105 Marietta Drive, Vestal, New York 13850, Telephone 607-722-0265 and 6251. Voice and FAX 607-722-0265.

ACKNOWLEDGMENTS

My sincere thanks to the following people for their contributions during the preparation of this book.

Paul D. Adomities, Baseball historian, writer, and editor for his help in identifying first basemen Duff Cooley of the 1900 Pittsburgh Pirates in one of the Postcards.

Don Bevans, President of All Star Cards for his excellent help during the preparation of the manuscript.

Donald R. Brown, Postcard authority and Assistant Director for Collection Management at the State Library of Pennsylvania for his help and advice.

Lee Cox, Postcard dealer who introduced me to Postcard artist Sherry Kemp and sold to me many of the Postcards that are illustrated in this book.

Roy Cox and John McClintock, who introduced me to the publisher of this book and sold many of the Postcards illustrated in this book to me.

Paul Dickson, author of *DICKSON'S BASEBALL DICTIONARY* who never failed to provide sound advice and generous help during the preparation of this book.

Elias J. Dudash, long time Postcard collector and traveling companion who generously permitted me to use Postcards from his outstanding collection as illustrations in this book.

The Late **Bill Fitzgerald**, whose untimely death caused me to lose a long-time friend, Baseball authority, and collecting colleague. He was an endless source of Baseball information.

Jerry M. Hermele, attorney and Postcard collecting colleague who provided advice throughout the preparation of this book.

Mike Hirsch, Postcard collecting colleague, who kindly loaned Postcards from his excellent collection for use as illustrations in this book.

Sherry Kemp, internationally known Postcard artist who provided the artwork for the author's personal Postcard.

William B. Mead, Baseball author who provided help and encouragement during the prepartion of this book.

Bill Price, who provided many of the Postcards for the illustrations used in this book.

Harvey N. Roehl, for his careful review and editing of the final text.

Glen B. Ruh, editor of Redefinition's *WORLD OF BASEBALL* who generously provided help and advice during the preparation of this book.

Tomoko Sano, Instructor, Japanese Language Dept. at the University of Maryland, for translating the legend on the Postcard showing Babe Ruth during his tour of Japan in 1934.

George Tinker, long-time Postcard collector, who introduced me to the joys of collecting Postcards more than 20 years ago.

Mike Walsh, who generously loaned some of the Postcards for use as illustrations in this book.

Dianna and Bob Weiner, for their excellent editing of the page proofs for this book.

PREFACE

Two of America's favorite pastimes are enjoying Baseball and collecting Picture Postcards. The combination of the two activities provides us with a fascinating historical study. This book is not an attempt to supply a complete history of either subject although, hopefully, you will be better informed about both subjects when you have examined this work.

Professional Baseball began in 1869 when the Cincinnati Red Stockings became the first professional team, and they completed an entire year without losing a game. Postcards were initially produced in the United States for the 1893 Columbian Exposition Worlds Fair, in Chicago. Soon after the Worlds Fair, the sending of Postcards became a favorite method of communicating with family and friends. Printed Color Picture Postcards began to appear in the major cities of the U.S., showing scenes of the more prominent sites in the area. In the smaller towns, where elaborately prepared Postcards were not economically feasible, local drugstores frequently sold Photographic Postcards depicting areas of interest including Main Street, stores, the town's baseball team, and ball park. People were able to take photographs of family, friends, and other subjects and have them made into Postcards by the local druggist.

The Postcard, as an inexpensive and rapid means of communication between people, usually has, on one side, a small space for a message, the address, and postage stamp(s). And on the other side there is a photograph or other form of reproduction of a "scene." The communication written on the Postcard may or may not be related to the scene. The writer may have used a Postcard showing a picture of a ball player to inquire about the activities and/or health of another member of the family or a friend.

Over a period of many years the Postcards were collected for the message, history, and the scene. As a result of these collecting interests we have a valuable source of information relating to many subjects, including Baseball, from a historical, technical, and artistic perspective. The Postcards shown in this book provide a chronological history of Baseball.

The majority of the better quality Color Postcards produced in the early 1900s were manufactured in Germany. German printing techniques were superior to the printing in other parts of the world until the beginning of World War I.

The Picture Postcard History of Baseball as described in this book begins in 1901 when an eight-team American League was established in competition with the National League. The National League was formed in 1876. This first decade of the twentieth century was also important to Baseball with the construction of the first modern steel and concrete ball parks in Philadelphia and Pittsburgh.

This book is a chronological display of the players, teams, and stadiums at the Major League level. The study ends in 1959 with the 16 Major League teams that existed before the expansion of the clubs. Baseball's "Age of Innocence" ended in the 1950s with the shift of five established teams (franchises) in Boston, St. Louis, Philadelphia, New York, and Brooklyn. They moved to provide better economic futures for themselves.

As a result, there has been a careful selection of the available scenes for this book. In some instances, only one reproduction of a particular scene was available to this writer, although other scenes must exist. The descriptive caption for each scene offers historical and technical information combined with the comments of many interested people (see ACKNOWLEDGMENTS and BIBLIOGRAPHY) and this writer. No claim is made to originality or completeness in the captions.

The reader will notice a greater emphasis on the earlier decades rather than the period from 1920 through 1949. This emphasis is not accidental. America was deeply involved in the Great Depression in the 1930s and World War II during the 1940s. The output of Postcards was sharply curtailed during those years. Also, from 1923, when Yankee Stadium was built, and 1932, when the Cleveland Municipal Stadium was completed, no new Major League stadiums were completed until the Milwaukee County Stadium was finished in 1953.

I am certain that many important players, teams, and stadiums are not included, either due to the fact that Postcards were not produced to illustrate these Baseball scenes or because I have not been able to acquire the Postcards. Hopefully, the owners of these Postcards will place some of them in circulation.

A NOTE TO THE DELTIOLIGISTS:

Five types of Postcards (produced by different printing techniques) are used to illustrate this book:

Prelinen	1900-1930
Linen	1930-1950
Chrome	1939-to date
Black & White	All dates
Real Photographic Cards	All dates

The Linen and Chrome periods overlap, as there are many examples of the same Postcard being produced using both printing techniques.

To provide reference information for your collection of these Postcards, the following information was taken from each Postcard and added below each illustration.

Publisher:	(Name and address of the publisher and Postcard No.)
Manufacturer:	(Name and address)
Type:	(Chrome, Black & White, Artist Color, Real Photograph, Linen, etc.)
Postmark:	(If the Postcard has been used, name of the town, state, and date)
Value Index:	(A single letter based on the following code)

- A = Very Rare
- B = Rare
- C = Fairly Rare
- D = Scarce
- E = Fairly Common
- F = Common
- G = Very Common

If any of these five items of information are not printed on either side of the Postcard then "Not Indicated" is shown below the illustration. There are listings that include all five items, some show one or more items, and some show none of the items.

With this information in mind, the author suggests that you sit back, relax, and enjoy traveling back in time to meet the players, teams, and see the stadiums that made Baseball the important drama that it was and formed the foundation of the great game of today.

INTRODUCTION

Baseball history through Picture Postcards. That's a great idea that Ron Menchine has developed. He has combined "Wish you were here" with "Take me out to the ball game." With careful thought we know that Ron is the man to create this book. A long-time Postcard collector he also has a varied background in sports—Baseball in particular. He has put together a book that every Baseball buff will enjoy, by using his vast collection of Postcards and his thorough knowledge of the game.

As you begin to read this book consider the many stadiums that you can visit, the players that you will meet, and the memories that you can evoke by looking through this outstanding collection of Postcards. Also, you can enjoy the history of Baseball that Ron has provided as you read through the captions that are included with each illustration. The Postcard collector will also find those extra fascinating pieces of information for their collections.

Actor, narrator, and sportscaster, Ron Menchine is a versatile man. I remember him best when he did an outstanding job as the voice of the Washington Senators back in the days when the national pastime was part of the nation's capitol. He has also been active as an announcer in professional and college football, basketball, soccer, and other sports.

I watched him in the movies. He appeared in the *Seduction of Joe Tynan* and *All of the Presidents Men*. He also played the part of an attorney in the TV series *The Adams Chronicles*.

With all of these accomplishments as background, my best image of Ron is a good friend and conversationalist. He is the world's greatest one-man audience; always ready with a good, hearty laugh for your joke or quip. In addition, he was always ready to help in any task including baby-sitter for my twin daughters when the Harwells lived in Baltimore, to helping me pack my Baseball collection when I left the Orioles to become the voice of the Tigers.

This old and true friend has now gone a large step forward in finding the right combination of Baseball's pictures and history in this new and unusual book. I know that you will agree that this journey through Baseball via the Picture Postcard route is something that you and I will enjoy for many years.

Ernie Harwell

Ernie Harwell

NOTE TO THE READER

The following abbreviations are used in this text:

BA   Batting Average

BH(s)   Base Hit(s)

ERA   Earned Run Average

HR(s)   Home Run(s)

RBI   Runs Batted In

The three nicely attired young men in this photograph hardly project the image of professional Baseball players; however, all were prominent members of the 1900 Pittsburgh Pirates. On the left is outfielder Tommy Leach, in the center is first baseman Duff Cooley and to the right Honus Wagner, one of the most famous and finest players in Baseball history. The Pirates of 1900 finished in second place, in the 12-team National League, 4-1/2 games behind the Brooklyn Dodgers. The year 1900 was the first time these players were members of the Pirates. Leach and Wagner had played with Louisville and continued to play for many seasons with the Pirates. Cooley formerly played with Philadelphia and he

Publisher: Not Indicated * Manufacturer: Not Indicated * Type: Real Photograph * Postmark: Not Used * Value Index: A

had only a .201 batting average (BA) for the season with the Pirates after which he was traded to Boston. This average was his lowest during a 13-year Major League career with a .294 lifetime BA. In 1900 Wagner had an outstanding season leading the National League with a .381 BA, the highest in his brilliant 21-year career.

"Winning my first batting title in 1900 was my greatest thrill in Baseball," Wagner recalled later. Although Honus attained his fame as a shortstop he played right field and did not make the transition to shortstop until 1901. Leach was a utility player at third base, shortstop, second base, and the outfield in 1900 playing in 51 games with a .213 BA. At the end of his 19-season career in 1918 he had a .269 lifetime BA. This extremely rare Postcard is the earliest-known Postcard featuring Major League Baseball players.

Many Baseball fans do not realize that the Baltimore Orioles were a charter member of the American League when play began in 1901.

The Orioles of today rejoined the American League when the financially troubled St. Louis Browns moved to Baltimore in 1954. The Orioles began favorably in the newly formed League. On April 26, 1901 an overflow crowd of 10,371 fans saw Manager John McGraw lead his team past the Boston Puritans (later the Red Sox) by a 10 to 6 score. Despite a fifth-place finish for the year, there were many highlights as McGraw had a .352 BA for the second-highest average in the league. "Iron Man" Joe McGinnity won 26 games, second to Cy Young of Boston who had 33 vic-

Publisher: Not Indicated * Manufacturer: Not Indicated * Type: Real Photograph * Postmark: Not Used * Value Index: A

tories. Unfortunately, in 1902 the team finished last, winning 50 and losing 88 games. They moved from Baltimore to New York City to become the Highlanders and later the Yankees. This photograph was taken during a heavyweight boxing match between Al Kaufman and Al Kubrick in 1909 and is the only known Postcard of this American League park. The Minor League Orioles took over the park in 1903 and it remained their home until 1916.

PHILADELPHIA - COLUMBIA BALL PARK.
2/23/07 Am Working hard — at the so how. — Ed —

Publisher: The World Postcard Co, Philadelphia, PA * Manufacturer: Not Indicated * Type: Black-White Photograph *
Postmark: Not Used * Value Index: A

In 1901 Ben Shibe and Connie Mack obtained a franchise for a Philadelphia team to be known as the Athletics in the new American League and they hurriedly sought a location for a ball park. In his autobiography *MY 66 YEARS IN THE BIG LEAGUES*, Connie Mack discusses the search. "We now had our franchise but we had no team and no park. What I learned about Philadelphia, I learned from walking the entire city, inspecting every vacant lot. We were in such a hurry to get started that we thought we might have to take a city playground. Finally we decided upon a site at 29th Street and Columbia Avenue and got it on a 10-year lease. Columbia Park is the name we gave it. We had just five weeks after leasing the park to put up the stands in order to keep the franchise. It didn't take us long to construct a single decked wooden grandstand." Columbia Park, in a section of Philadelphia called Brewerytown, was ready for the opening game on April 24, 1901. Actually, two days of rain delayed the official opening until April 26th, and an overflow crowd of more than 10,000 people watched the Athletics lose to the Washington Senators by a 5 to 1 score. However, the Athletics' second baseman, Napoleon Lajoie, who had been induced (for more money) by Messers Shibe and Mack to jump from the National League Phillies was the hitting star in a losing cause. He had three hits in that game. Lajoie's batting exploits were a portent of things to come as he led the American League with a remarkable .426 BA. The League's second-leading hitter, Mike Donlin of Baltimore, had a .340 BA. LaJoie was obviously head and shoulders above everyone else and led the American League with 14 home runs (HRs) and 125 runs batted in (RBI), becoming the League's first Triple Crown Winner. The Athletics finished fourth during 1901. They were American League Champions in 1902. However, no World Series was played with the National League Champions as the American League had raided many National League teams and created much animosity in the older league. The differences were resolved in 1903 and the first World Series was played that year between the American League Champion Boston Puritans (Red Sox) and the National League champion Pittsburgh Pirates.

The Cleveland League Park had a rich heritage. Built for the Cleveland Spiders of the National League in 1891, it served as their home until 1899 when they lost their franchise. When Cleveland was awarded a charter membership in the American League in 1901, League Park became their home grounds. Trolley magnate Frank Robison selected the site at 66th Street and Lexington Avenue because it was on his streetcar line and easily accessible to the fans. In 1892 the Spiders won the Pennant during the first half while the Boston Red Stockings were second-half victors. The Spiders met in a post season series with Boston, winning five straight games. In game one, the teams battled to an 11-inning, 0-0 score in game one, a duel between

Publisher: Not Indicated * Manufacturer: Not Indicated * Type: Real Photograph * Postmark: Not Used * Value Index A

Cleveland's Cy Young and Boston's Kid Nichols. Cleveland finished second to the champion Orioles in 1895 and 1896 and played them for the League Championship trophy called the Temple Cup which was donated by Pittsburgh sportsman Col. William Temple. The Spiders upset the Orioles four games to one in 1895 and lost to them in four straight games in 1896. League Park served its tenants well but it was obvious in 1909 that the wooden structure was no longer suitable. A modern League Park of concrete and steel was built on the same site, in time for the opening game of the 1910 season.

Bennett Park was named after Charley Bennett, one of the heroes of the Detroit Wolverines' victory over the St. Louis Browns in the 1887 World Series. The games matched the National League champion Wolverines against the Browns who were champions of the American Association (a major league from 1882 through 1891). Detroit fans were so enthralled with Bennett's performance that they rewarded the popular catcher with a wheelbarrow containing 520 Silver Dollars at the conclusion of the final game. Charley was a popular figure around Detroit for many years. He lost both legs in a train accident in 1894. Detroit's new ball park at Michigan and

Publisher: Not Indicated * Manufacturer: Not Indicated * Type: Real Photograph * Postmark: Not Used * Value Index: A

Trumbull Avenues was named in his honor when the city was awarded a franchise in the fledgling American League in 1901. The team was known as the Tigers. Bennett Park served as the Tigers' home from the first season of 1901 through the 1911 season. The site at Michigan and Trumbull Avenues remains the location of Detroit's ball park, now known as Tiger Stadium. Bennett Park had an illustrious history as the Tigers won American League championships in 1907, 1908, and 1909 but always failed to win the World Series. In this only known photograph of Bennett Park used on a Postcard, Detroit area youngsters and their teams are shown parading around the field before a Tigers game. Despite his tragic accident, Charley Bennett was a frequent spectator at Tiger games until his death in 1927.

When floodwaters ravaged the Pittsburgh area in 1902, photographs and Postcards were prepared to record the area scenes including the height of the rising water outside of Exposition Park. When the Allegheny River was at its peak, on July 4, the Pittsburgh Pirates were scheduled for a doubleheader with the Brooklyn Superbas. More than 10,000 fans were there despite at least one foot of water in the outfield. They played the games and all balls hit to the outfield were automatic singles. The Pirates won the morning game by a 3 to 0 score. By afternoon the water had crept to within 20 feet of second base. Undaunted, the Pirate management continued to play ball and hired youngsters to dry off the baseball after every pitch. By playing the double-header under the adverse conditions the Pirates gained two more wins and the money from the gate receipts.

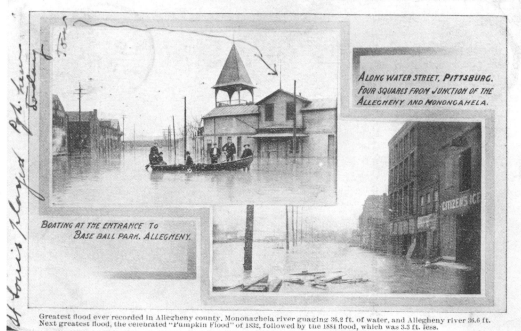

ALONG WATER STREET, PITTSBURG. FOUR SQUARES FROM JUNCTION OF THE ALLEGHENY AND MONONGAHELA.

BOATING AT THE ENTRANCE TO BASE BALL PARK, ALLEGHENY.

Greatest flood ever recorded in Allegheny county. Monongahela river guaging 36.2 ft. of water, and Allegheny river 36.6 ft. Next greatest flood, the celebrated "Pumpkin Flood" of 1832, followed by the 1884 flood, which was 3.3 ft. less.

Publisher: Publishers Circulation Promotion Association, Pittsburgh, PA * Manufacturer: Not Indicated * Type: Black & White * Postmark: Not Used * Value Index: C

American League President Ban Johnson was anxious to put a franchise in New York because he knew a team in the nation's largest city would bring the new league instant credibilitiy. When the American League was founded in 1901 it had franchises in Baltimore, Boston, Chicago, Cleveland, Detroit, Milwaukee, Philadelphia and Washington. In 1902 the members remained the same with the exception of Milwaukee, whose franchise was moved to St. Louis. In the 1902 American League season the Baltimore Orioles were in last place and in financial difficulty. President Johnson was able to switch the franchise to New York. The Baltimore franchise was purchased for $18,000 by two New Yorkers, Frank Farrell and Bill Devery. They found a

American League Base Ball Park, New York.

Publisher: Thaddeus Wilkerson, New York, NY * Manufacturer: Thaddeus Wilkerson * Type: Real Photograph * Postmark: Not Used * Value Index: A

playing site on Broadway between 165th and 168th Streets and hastily constructed a wooden ball park which became known as Hilltop Park because of the high elevation. John W. Gordon was brought in by the owners to operate the team as president and because of his last name, someone thought of the famous British military unit known as Gordon Highlanders. Based on these names and Hilltop Park's location, "Highlanders" was selected as the team's name. Hilltop Park opened on May 1, 1903 with the Highlanders beating the Washington Senators by an 8 to 1 score before an overflow crowd of 16,293. This photograph by Thaddeus Wilkerson shows the wooden grandstand as it looked from center field. The water you see in the background is the Hudson River.

Polo Grounds, New York.

Publisher: Thaddeus Wilkerson, New York, NY * Manufacturer: Thaddeus Wilkerson * Type: Real Photo * Postmark: Not Used * Value Index:A

The Polo Grounds is a funny name for a baseball park and there is an interesting story behind it. When Troy Haymaker's franchise was shifted to New York City in 1883, the new team needed a playing site. Team owner John B. Day made arrangements to use the polo field, owned by New York Herald publisher James Gordon Bennett, located at 110th Street and 5th Avenue. The name became synonymous with baseball in New York, and every future home of the Metropolitans (later known as the Giants) became the Polo Grounds. The Players League came into existence in 1890 and the owners built their stadium next to the existing home of the Giants. It was called Brotherhood Park, as the Players League was run by the players themselves. However, their business skills were no match for those of the established National League owners and the Players League ended after one season. The park was more modern than the one used by the Giants and they moved into Brotherhood Park, which was rechristened the Polo Grounds. The park remained their home until it burned down on April 13, 1911. This rare Thaddeus Wilkerson Postcard shows the wooden park originally built for the Players League. It was the site of the 1905 World Series, where Christy Mathewson pitched the third of his shutouts in leading the Giants to a four-games-to-one triumph over the Philadelphia Athletics.

1903 was John McGraw's first full season as manager of the New York Giants and he skillfully guided them into second place after they had finished in last place in 1902. This Postcard is the earliest known view showing a Major League Team and uses the grand setting of the staircase at New York's famous Waldorf Astoria Hotel as the background. Baseball had an image problem in the early years as many of the players were hard-drinking rowdies and teams stayed in second-class hotels. Being associated with one of the world's finest hotels, such as the Waldorf Astoria, gave them more respectability. McGraw had learned his managing craft as one of the stars of the famous Baltimore Orioles of the 1890s, and he was years ahead of his contemporaries as a strategist and innovator. As was the case with many of McGraw's future Giant teams, pitching was their strength. Righthander "Iron Man" Joe McGinnity, second from the left in the second row, led the National League with 32 wins while Christy Mathewson, seated next to McGinnity on his right, was the League's second leading pitcher with 29 victories. McGinnity and Mathewson were eventually elected to Baseball's Hall of Fame. Another future Hall-of-Famer, Roger Bresnahan, who led the 1903 Giants in batting with a .350 BA is sitting by himself in the bottom row.

Publisher: Photo by Falk, New York, NY * Manufacturer: Photo by Falk * Type: Real Photograph * Postmark: Not Used * Value Index: A

Publisher: I. & M. Ottenheimer, Baltimore, MD * Manufacturer: Not Indicated * Type: Black & White * Postmark: Nov. 20, 1906 Traverse City, Michigan * Value Index: C

In 1903, when the first World Series in 1903 shifted from Boston to Pittsburgh, the Pirates played their games at this home field.

Located at the confluence of the Allegheny and Monongahela Rivers, Exposition Park was near the Three Rivers Stadium site used by the Pirates today. As you can see in this photograph taken from a nearby hill, the fans could gather there and look into the ball park free of charge. For big events such as the 1903 World Series, they frequently watched the action from the hill. In the four games played at Exposition Park during that first World Series, the Pirates had crowds of 7,600, 12,322, 11,556 and 17,038, the latter being the second-largest crowd in Pirate history at this historic ball park. However, this large and enthusiastic crowd could not alter the results and the Boston Puritans defeated the Pirates by a 7 to 3 score as Cy Young outpitched Deacon Phillippe. The Puritans upset the Pirates in that initial World Series five games to three. Exposition Park served as the Pirates' home from 1891 until 1909 and was resurrected in 1914 when the Federal League Rebels used it for two seasons before the Federal League collapsed because of financial difficulties.

Although the American League was founded in 1901, 1903 was the first year that the champions of the American League and National League met in a World Series. Pittsburgh owner Barney Dreyfuss sought out Boston owner Harry Killea in August when it became apparent that his Pirates and the Puritans (later Red Sox) would win their respective League championships. He suggested a best-five-games-out-of-nine series. A World Series had been played in the 1880s and 1890s by the champions from the National League and rival American Association. When the American Association was absorbed into the National League in 1892 the top two teams met in what was called the Temple Cup Series. No series had

Publisher: Not Indicated * Manufacturer: Not Indicated * Type: Real Photograph * Postmark: Not Used * Value Index: A

taken place since 1897 when the Baltimore Orioles defeated the Boston Beaneaters four games to one in the final Temple Cup Series. The wooden structure shown above is Boston's Huntington Avenue Grounds, site of the first game of the modern World Series. The Pirates led by Player-Manager Fred Clarke and incomparable shortstop Honus Wagner had won their third straight National League Pennant and were heavy favorites over the upstart Puritans. 16,242 fans crammed into the Puritans ball park (made to hold approximately 8,500) and most went away disappointed as 28-game winner Cy Young gave up four first-inning runs and was clearly outpitched by Deacon Phillippe. The Pirates won by a 7 to 3 score. Despite falling behind three games to one, the Puritans captured four games of the next five as Young had two victories and Bill Dineen recorded three wins. Phillippe was magnificent in a losing cause, gaining all three Pirates victories. The Boston Puritans were champions of the world.

This photograph of the 1904 New York Giants shows the first of Manager John McGraw's teams to win a National League Pennant. With Christy Mathewson winning 34 games, Joe McGinnity capturing 33 victories, and Dummy Taylor gaining 22 wins, pitching continued to be the team's main attribute. They ended the season with 106 wins and only 47 losses, good enough for a 13-game lead over second place Chicago. Surprisingly, not one Giant regular had a .300 BA during that season and utility man Jack Dunn topped the batters with a .309 BA. With the strength of McGraw's pitching staff, good hitting was obviously not necessary in order for the Giants to win. Shortstop Bill Dahlen did lead the National League with 80 RBI while left fielder Sam Mertes was third in the League with

Publisher: The Rotograph Co. New York, NY * Manufacturer: The Rotograph Co * Type: Real Photograph * Postmark: Rochester, NY November 18, 1905 * Value Index: A

78 RBI. Note that the portrait of John McGraw dominates this photograph of the 1904 Giants. His brilliant managing was the primary force behind the team and although great players would come and go, McGraw's managerial skill nearly always kept the Giants in the thick of the Pennant race. He won 10 National League Championships before retiring in 1932. The only negative surrounding this outstanding 1904 Giant team was that McGraw and owner John Brush refused to play the American League's Boston Puritans, who repeated as champions, in the World Series. That situation changed in 1905.

New York Giants Manager John McGraw always felt that Christy Mathewson was the greatest pitcher he had ever seen, but he rated righthander Joe McGinnity in the top echelon of all-time great pitchers. In his autobiography, MY THIRTY YEARS IN BASEBALL, McGraw said about McGinnity, "He was pretty nearly as good as Matty. Joe had pretty nearly everything a pitcher needs including a puzzling underhand ball and a baffling change of pace." McGinnity did not get his nickname "Iron Man" because he pitched and won both games of a doubleheader on three occasions. The name was given to him because he worked in an iron foundry during his off seasons. In only 10 seasons in the Major Leagues, he won 242 games against 142 losses, an average of more than 24 victories a year. Breaking in with the Baltimore Orioles in 1899 Joe won 28 games during his first year to lead all National League pitchers. To prove his winning was not beginner's luck, McGinnity won 28 games during the 1900 season pitching for Brooklyn with more wins than any National League pitcher. When the American League was organized in 1901, he left the National League to join John McGraw who was in charge of the Baltimore American League team. He won 24 games with the Orioles, finishing second to Boston's Cy Young who led the American League with 33 victories. In 1902, when McGraw left the Orioles to become manager of the New York Giants, McGinnity jumped back to the National League to join him. With the Giants in 1903 he won 32 games, more than any National League pitcher, and won his career high of 33 victories in 1904. "Iron Man" Joe McGinnity was unquestionably one of the finest pitchers of all time and was elected to the Baseball Hall of Fame in 1946.

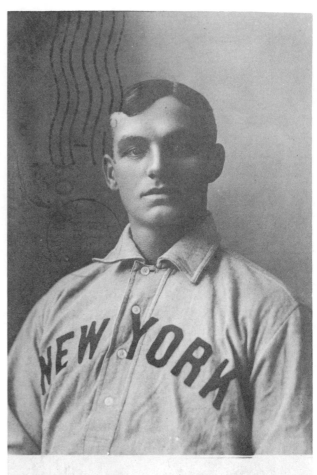

JOSEPH McGINNITY

Remember me to all *your truly* *m. & D.*

Publisher: The Rotograph Co * Manufacturer: The Rotograph Co * Type: Real Photograph * Postmark: Brooklyn, NY August 13, 1907 * Value Index: A

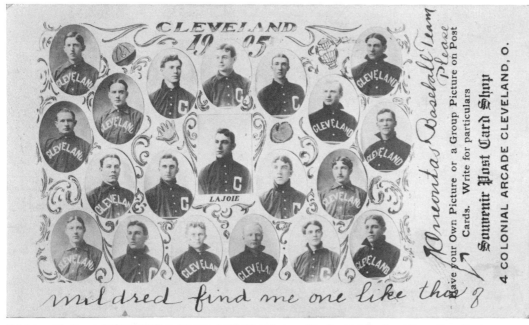

mildred find me one like that

Publisher: The Souvenir Postcard Shop, Cleveland, OH * Manufacturer: The Souvenir Postcard Shop * Type: Real Photograph * Postmark: Cleveland, OH June 3, 1907 * Value Index: A

Napoleon Lajoie performed brilliantly in the Major Leagues for 21 years, mainly as a second baseman and he had a unique distinction. He was the only player in Major League history to have a team named after him. When Cleveland was a member of the National League in the 1890s, the team was called the Spiders. Then in 1901 when Cleveland became a charter member of the rival American League, the first team was called the Blues. In 1902 they were referred to as the Broncos, but like Blues, the nickname never caught on with fans. A Cleveland newspaper conducted a poll among fans to select a new name and they voted overwhelmingly to call the team the Naps in honor of their outstanding second baseman.

Napoleon Lajoie came to Cleveland during the 1902 season and established himself immediately as the fans' choice with a .379 BA. He remained Cleveland's star player for 12 seasons and managed the ball club for five seasons with moderate success. With Lajoie as manager from 1905 through 1909, the Naps won 397 games while losing 330. The team's best season under Lajoie was 1908 when they finished in second place, only one-half game behind the Detroit Tigers, managed by Hughie Jennings.

This 1905 photograph shows Napoleon Lajoie in his first season as Naps' manager surrounded by his team which finished in fifth place in the American League with a record of 76 wins and 78 losses.

The 1905 Philadelphia Athletics were a fine baseball team. Managed adroitly by Connie Mack, the Athletics won 92 and lost 56 games. Top heavy in pitching talent, the 1905 Athletics had three 20-game winners, and had no batters above a .284 BA (compiled by Team Captain Harry Davis). Lefthander Eddie Plank, third from the left in the middle row of this photograph, was the American League's top pitcher with a record of 26 wins and only 12 losses. Eccentric Rube Waddell, one of baseball's most famous "characters" pictured third from the right in the top row with arms folded, had the League's best ERA of 1.48 with a record of 24 wins and 11 losses. Righthander Andy Coakley enjoyed his finest Major League season with 20 wins and 6 defeats which gave him the league's best 769 pitching percentage.

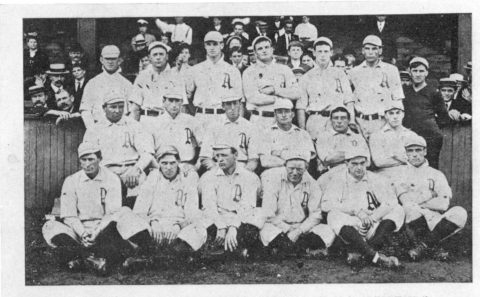

PHILADELPHIA AMERICAN LEAGUE BASE BALL TEAM ["ATHLETICS"]
Reading from left to right are: Top row Murphy, Davis, Hanley, Waddell Knight, Bender. Midd'e row-Seybold, Coakley, Plank, L. Cross, Schreck. Lord, Lower row-M Cross, Hoffman, Barton, Hartsel, Dygert, Powers

Publisher: Not Indicated * Manufacturer: Not Indicated * Type: Black & White * Postmark: Not Used * Value Index: B

In order to save money during the early days of baseball the teams frequently made two players share a single bed. Catcher Ossee Schreckengost ("Schreck"), seated second from the right in the middle row, required a clause written into his contract that roommate Rube Waddell not be allowed to eat animal crackers in bed. As great as the Athletic pitchers were, the New York Giant pitchers proved to be better in the 1905 World Series. Giant pitchers did not allow a single earned run and they won the World Series four games to one. Christy Mathewson pitched three Shutouts for New York while Joe McGinnity pitched one. Philadelphia's only win came on Chief Bender's four-hit shutout in the second game by a 3 to 0 score with all three Philadelphia runs being unearned as a result of two Giant errors.

If the New York Giants were afraid to play the American League champion Boston Puritans in the 1904 World Series, they more than made up for it in 1905. John McGraw candidly admitted in his autobiography, MY THIRTY YEARS IN BASEBALL that Giants owner John Brush "Did not see why we should jeopardize the fruits of our victory by recognizing and playing against the champions of an organization (American League) that had been formed to put us out of business." In the first World Series in 1903 the American League Puritans stunned the Baseball world by upsetting the National League champion Pittsburgh Pirates. However, in 1905 peace between the Leagues had been restored and the Giants

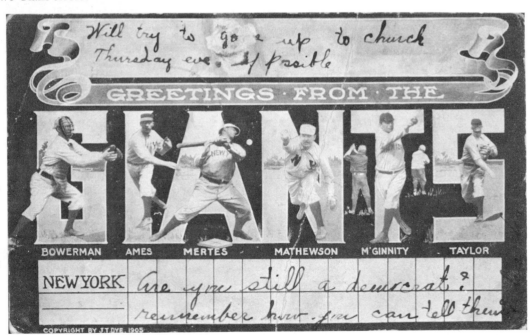

Publisher: J.T. Dye, New York, NY * Manufacturer: Not Indicated * Type: Black & White * Postmark: Roland, PA, April 11, 1907 * Value Index: B

made amends for their reticence of 1904. The Giants' 105 wins was close to the 108 games they had won in 1904. Again Christy Mathewson was a 30-game winner, registering 32 victories against only 8 losses to lead the National League. Mathewson also compiled the League's best 1.27 ERA. Mike Donlin in his first year as a Giants outfielder led the team with a .336 BA, third best in the National League. The Giants were the toast of New York and this photograph shows a few of the stars. Of the six players shown four are pitchers, and all of them righthanders. Red Ames recorded 22 wins, Joe McGinnity had 21 victories, and Dummy Taylor won 15 games. Left fielder Sam Mertes, to the left of Mathewson, led the Giants with 108 RBI. Sam Bowerman on the extreme left, shared catching duties with future Hall-of-Famer Roger Bresnahan, and he had a .269 BA and 41 RBI. The 1905 World Series against the Philadelphia Athletics was the only Series in history where all games ended in shutouts.

9

First baseman Dan McGann was an integral part of the World Champion New York Giants in 1905 and a better-than-average ball player who enjoyed a 13-year Major League career. Born in Shelbyville, KY he joined the Louisville Colonels of the National League as a 22-year-old infielder in 1895 and finished his career with the Boston Braves in 1908. McGann was a particular favorite of Giants manager John McGraw, who was Dan's teammate with the Baltimore Orioles in 1898. McGann had a .301 BA in 1898 and 106 RBI while playing first base for the Orioles who finished second to Boston in the National League standings. In 1902 McGraw was managing the American League Orioles when after 62 games, he suddenly jumped to the National League to manage the New York Giants. He left the Orioles in difficulty and had McGann leave Baltimore to join him in New York. McGann was batting .316 in 68 games at the time of his departure so it was a critical blow to the Orioles, who finished the season in last place in the American League. They were sold to New York investors at the end of the season, became the Highlanders, and then the Yankees. During the Giants' world championship season of 1905, McGann had a .299 BA and 75 RBI to finish third among the Giants trailing Sam Mertes, who had 108 RBI, and Bill Dahlen, with 81 RBI. This photograph shows Dan McGann as a base runner at first base. Note that he is wearing a uniform that proudly proclaims the Giants as World Champions.

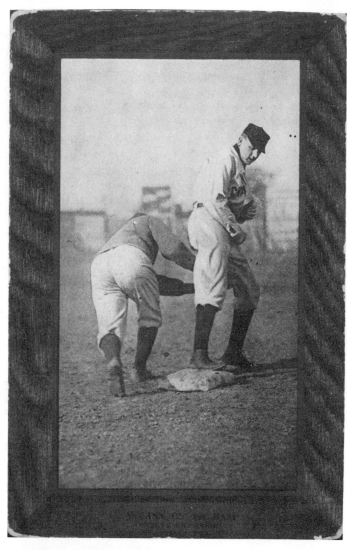

Publisher: The Ullman Manufacturing Co., New York, NY * Manufacturer: The Ullman Manufacturing Co * Type: Black & White * Postmark: Not Used * Value Index : A

M. BROWN.   J. PFEISTER   A. HOFMAN   C. G. WILLIAMS   O. OVERALL.   E. REULBACH.   J. KLING.
H. GESSLER.   J. TAYLOR.   H. STEINFELDT.   J. McCORMICK   F. CHANCE.   J. SHECKARD.   P. MORAN.   F. SCHULTE
C. LUNDGREN.   T. WALSH.   J. EVERS   J. SLAGLE.   J. TINKER.
CHICAGO NATIONAL LEAGUE BALL CLUB 1906   THE "CUBS"—PENNANT WINNERS

Publisher: Not Indicated * Manufacturer: Not Indicated * Type: Black & White * Postmark: Chicago, IL, October 16, 1906 * Value Index: C

The 1906 Chicago Cubs were unquestionably one of the greatest teams in baseball history. A team that included their famous stonewall infield, Frank Chance at first base, Johnny Evers at second base, Joe Tinker at shortstop and Harry Steinfeld at third base. Tinker, Evers, and Chance all made it to the Baseball Hall of Fame. In 1906 Steinfeld had an outstanding .327 BA. "Three Finger" Brown with 25 victories, Ed Reulbach with 20 wins, and Jake Pfeister with 19 victories, led a brilliant pitching staff. Manager Frank Chance, known as the "Peerless Leader," is seated in the middle row, fourth from the right. Shortstop Joe Tinker is seated on the far right-hand side of the first row and Second Baseman Johnny Evers is one person away from Tinker in the center of the bottom row. Although the 1906 Cubs lost in the World Series, using virtually the same team in 1907 and 1908 they won both the National League Pennant and the World Series.

The 1906 Chicago White Sox were called "The Hitless Wonders" and for good reason. They had the lowest BA in the American League, a paltry .230. However, they won the American League Pennant by three games over the second place New York Highlanders. Nick Altrock, second from the left in the bottom row of this photograph (who later gained fame as a baseball clown), led the way with 21 victories. He was followed closely by Ed Walsh and Frank Owen each with 19 wins, and Doc White, with 18 victories and a League best ERA of 1.52. Despite pitching brilliance, they were given no chance against their crosstown rivals, the Chicago Cubs, in the 1906 World Series. The Cubs had stampeded to the National League Pennant, winning 116 and losing 36

WHITE SOX -- 1906 TEAM

COPYRIGHTED, 1906, BY F. P. BURKE

Reading from left to right the players are: (Top row) Hart, McFarland, Davis, President Comiskey, Isbell, Sullivan and White. (Middle row) Walsh, Smith, Roth, Hahn, Dundon, Donohue, O'Neill, Tannehill and Rohe. (Lower row) Towne, Altrock, Owen, Patterson, Dougherty, Jones and Fiene.

Publisher:F.P. Burke Chicago, IL * Manufacturer: Not Indicated * Type: Black & White * Postmark: Chicago, IL October 15, 1906 * Value Index: B

games, a record that remains to date, and finished 20 games in front of the second-place New York Giants who were the defending World Champions. Despite the huge odds against them, the White Sox captured Major League Baseball's first intercity series by winning four games to two. Future Hall-of-Famer Ed Walsh was the World Series pitching hero for the White Sox, as he won two games, while Altrock and White each won one game. Walsh is shown here on the far left-hand side of the middle row and White is at the end of the top row on the right-hand side. White Sox owner Charles A. Comiskey is wearing the suit and hat in the middle of the top row.

"Palace of the Fans." Just the name conjures up an image of the ultimate in ball parks and this Cincinnati ball park was exactly that magnificent when it opened in 1902. For the fans' convenience, there were two bars below the stands that sold whiskey and beer. After having a few drinks, the imbibers would retire to their seats below the main grandstand along both foul lines. This area was called "Rooters Row" and you can imagine what choice comments would result from the section during the course of the game. The ball park received its name from the wooden columns and pillars which were copied from buildings (called palaces) at the 1893 Columbian Exposition. That design was the architectural style of the day; however, as a

Publisher: The Morgan Stationary Co, Cincinnati, OH * Manufacturer: Not Indicated * Type: Pre-Linen * Postmark: Not Used * Value Index: A

wooden structure it had a susceptibility to fire. In the fall of 1911 fire destroyed a large section of the grandstand and it was rebuilt on the same location, using steel and concrete. The columns and pillars were no longer the architectural vogue and when the new ball park opened in 1912, the columns and pillars were missing from Redland Field. This photograph, revealing all the splendors of the Palace of the Fans, was taken at the opening game of the 1907 season. It was not a good year for the Reds, who finished sixth in the National League with a record of 66 wins and 87 defeats.

The scene depicted on this Postcard showing ball players arriving at the Cincinnati Baseball Grounds by a horse-drawn buggy typified the game in the early 1900s. The buggy was the preferred method of transporting teams to the ball park as motorized vehicles were relatively new on the American scene. This photograph shows the exterior of the Palace of the Fans. As you saw, in the previous photograph showing the park's interior, it was a beautiful structure architecturally because the columns used to support the roof gave the park a palatial appearance. Although the Palace of the Fans contained many creature comforts for the fans, there were no clubhouses for the players.

Ball Players entering Cincinnati Grounds, ready for Game.

Publisher: Kraemer Art Co, Cincinnati, OH * Manufacturer: Not Indicated * Type: Pre-Linen * Postmark: Bluffton, IN, January 25, 1909 * Value Index: A

Both teams had to dress elsewhere and fully uniformed players arrived at the park by public and private conveyance. The players in full uniform were at the mercy of youngsters who took great delight in pelting them with mud, fruit, and vegetables. Obviously when Redland Field was built in 1912 containing modern clubhouses, players were delighted that they were no longer exposed to the fans. During the tenure of the Reds in the Palace of the Fans, a third-place finish in 1904 was the best record they could achieve over their ten-year history in the ball park.

"Wee-Ah" was the battle cry of Detroit Tigers manager Hughie Jennings as he encouraged his team from his spot in the third base coaching box. The rally call seemed to work because they won three consecutive American League Pennants in 1907, 1908, and 1909. Jennings would pull up fistfuls of grass from around the coach's box, raise his left foot, and with clenched fists shout as loud as he could "wee-ah" or "ee-yah." His antics made him a crowd attraction. Hughie was born in the coal mining town of Pittston, Pennsylvania on April 2, 1870 and began his professional career with the Allentown, Pennsylvania team as a catcher. He joined Louisville, a member of the National League, in 1891, after impressing manager Jack Chapman while playing against Louisville in an exhibition game. At Louisville he was switched to first base and later to shortstop where he gained his greatest fame. The most important event that happened to Jennings was being traded to the Baltimore Orioles in 1892. He became one of the most important members of the famous Orioles who won National League Pennants in 1894, 1895 and 1896. As the Oriole shortstop, Jennings had a .335 BA in 1984, a .386 BA in 1895 and a .401 BA in 1896. Although the Orioles had a reputation of being the rowdiest and toughest players in baseball during the 1890s, Jennings was a warm friendly person with laughing blue eyes and a marvelous sense of humor that endeared him to everyone.

Publisher: Not Indicated * Manufacturer: Not Indicated * Type: Black & White * Postmark: Not Used * Value Index: B

If "Big Ed" Walsh had not injured his throwing arm during the 1913 season with the Chicago White Sox, we can only guess as to how many games the 6-foot-1-inch, 193-pound righthander would have won in the Major Leagues. Prior to the injury, Walsh had won 26 games in 1911 and 27 games in 1912. After the injury Walsh won only 5 and lost 5 games in four seasons. His Major League career totals show 194 wins against 130 losses. When John McGraw ranked the top pitchers of all time in his book, MY THIRTY YEARS IN BASEBALL, the Giants manager included "Big Ed." According to McGraw, "Walsh was easily the most famous and effective of all the spitball pitchers. A big factor in his value to a team was his marvelous endurance. Aside from

Publisher: George W. Hull, Chicago, IL * Manufacturer: Not Indicated * Type: Black & White * Postmark: Chicago, IL, September 21, 1907 * Value Index: B

his spitball Walsh had tremendous speed and splendid control." In the 1906 World Series Walsh won his two starts striking out 17 Cubs batters in 15 innings. In this photograph Ed Walsh displays the form that made him one of the best pitchers who ever played Baseball. Despite his injury-shortened career, "Big Ed" Walsh was inducted into the Baseball Hall of Fame in 1946.

Fate sometimes plays a cruel role in the success or failure of great athletes. Orval Overall, a pitcher for the Chicago Cubs is an example. In 1907 the big 6-foot-2-inch, 214-pound righthander, a former Baseball and Football star at the University of California, was the toast of the Baseball world. He was the National League's top pitcher with 23 victories and led the Cubs to their second consecutive Pennant. His ERA was a brilliant 1.70. In 1908, as the Cubs won their third National League Pennant, Overall won 17 and lost 11 while compiling another outstanding 1.92 ERA. Although the Cubs did not win the Pennant in 1909, Overall was exceptional, winning 21 games and losing 11 while compiling a 1.42 ERA, the best of his career. It

Publisher: G.F. Grignon, Chicago, IL * Manufacturer: Not Indicated * Type: Pre-Linen * Postmark: Chicago, IL, March 23, 1908 * Value Index: B

was more of the same in 1910 as Orval was on the way to his finest season. Midway in the year he had won 12 and lost 6 when he developed arm trouble. It seemed that his career was over. He was out of baseball for three years due to the sore arm and made a gallant attempt to come back in 1913. Unfortunately, after a lackluster record of four wins and four losses and a career high 3.31 ERA, Overall decided to retire. His Major League career was only seven seasons, during which time he had won 110 games and lost only 69 with an ERA of 2.24. He was in four different World Series with the Cubs with three wins and one loss. His only World Series defeat was in 1910 when his arm was virtually useless. We can safely assume that a continuation of his outstanding performances would have earned him a spot in the Hall of Fame. As it is, his chief claim to fame is being pictured on this highly prized Postcard honoring the champion Cubs of 1907.

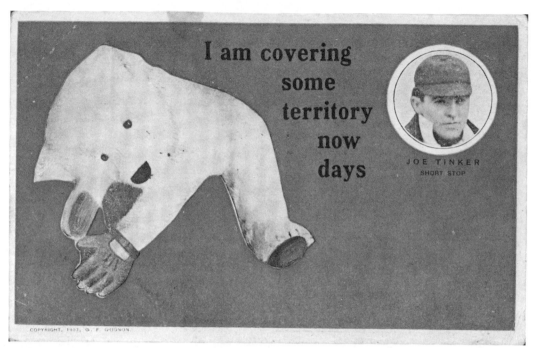

Publisher: G.F. Grignon Chicago, IL * Manufacturer: Not Indicated * Type: Pre-Linen * Postmark: Not Used * Value Index: B

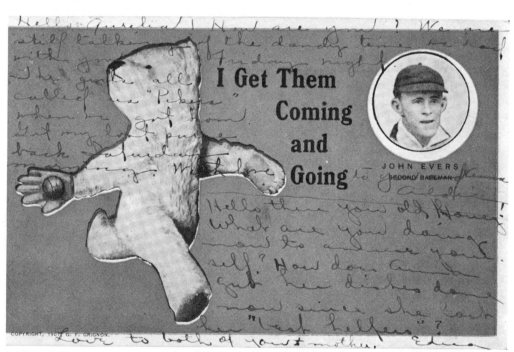

Publisher: G.F. Grignon Chicago, IL * Manufacturer: Not Indicated * Type: Pre-Linen * Postmark: Lansing, MI January 27, 1908 * Value Index: B

Franklin P. Adams never played an inning of professional Baseball. As a noted newspaper columnist for the *New York Evening Mail*, his contribution to the game will forever be part of Baseball lore. A strong New York Giants fan, Adams became increasingly frustrated when his beloved team would frequently suffer heartbreaking defeats playing the Chicago Cubs. The Cubs double-play combination of second baseman Johnny Evers and shortstop Joe Tinker continually distressed him with superb fielding plays and double plays that snuffed out rallies by the Giants. Cubs manager Frank Chance played first base and was on the receiving end of balls thrown to complete the rally ending double plays. Adams took out his disappointment over Giants' defeats on his typewriter and wrote "Baseball's Sad Lexicon," one of the most famous poems ever written about America's pastime.

> These are the saddest of possible words—
> Tinker to Evers to Chance
> Trio of bear Cubs and fleeter than birds,
> Tinker to Evers to Chance
> Thoughtlessly pricking' our gonfallon bubble
> Making a Giant hit into a double,
> Words that are weighty with nothing but trouble
> Tinker to Evers to Chance."

Frank Chance would have made the Baseball Hall of Fame playing in any era. In 17 seasons he had a lifetime .296 BA and despite his size (6 feet, 190 pounds) twice led the National League in stolen bases with 67 in 1903 and 57 in 1906. Although Johnny Evers and Joe Tinker were outstanding players in their own right, many Baseball historians say that Franklin Adams through his poem immortalized them forever and was instrumental in having them elected to the Baseball Hall of Fame. For the record, second baseman Johnny Evers had a career .270 BA over 18 seasons while shortstop Joe Tinker had a .262 BA over 15 seasons in the Major Leagues. In any event, Franklin P. Adams can share in their glory.

Publisher: H.M.Taylor, Detroit, MI * Manufacturer: Not Indicated * Type: Black & White * Postmark: Detroit, MI October 9, 1907 * Value Index: A

The Detroit Tigers won their first American League Pennant in 1907. It was also the year that Ty Cobb won his first of 12 American League batting championships. This photograph shows Ty Cobb at 20 years of age and already considered a star. Cobb batted .350 in winning his first batting championship and drove in 119 runs during the 1907 season. Despite this outstanding record, Cobb managed to improve it in later years. When he retired in 1928 as a player with the Philadelphia Athletics, his 24-year career showed a lifetime .367 BA, the highest average in Baseball history. In his final season, at age 42, Cobb had a .323 BA. Three times during his brilliant career, Ty batted above .400 with a .420 in 1911, his career high. Ty Cobb is rated as the fiercest competitor in the history of the game and the greatest base stealer of his day. Rube Bressler of the Philadelphia Athletics pitched against Cobb beginning in 1914 and had this to say about his adversary. "Cobb had that terrible fire, that unbelievable drive. His determination was fantastic. I never saw anybody like him. It was his base. It was his game. Everything was his. The most feared man in the history of Baseball." If Ty Cobb had a major disappointment during his fabulous career, it was never playing on a team that won a World Series. Cobb played in only three World Series with the Tigers in 1907, 1908, and 1909 and Detroit lost all three series. During the 1936 balloting for induction to the Baseball Hall of Fame Ty Cobb had more votes than anyone including Babe Ruth. The "Georgia Peach" was truly a Baseball immortal.

Sam Crawford called "Wahoo Sam" because he was born in Wahoo, Nebraska in 1880, always played in the shadow of Ty Cobb. Despite this image, he managed to distinguish himself as a Hall-of-Famer. When Crawford and Cobb played together as Detroit Tiger outfielders for twelve seasons, it was Cobb who attracted most of the attention. Crawford played right field and his 18-year Major League career ended with a .309 BA and a reputation as one of the hardest hitters of the dead ball era. His record of 312 career triples stands as the all time best. Sam retired in 1917 before the use of the lively ball of the 1920s. If he had played during that era there is no telling how many HRs he might have hit. When he played for the Cincinnati Reds in 1901 he led the National League with 16 HRs and 104 RBI, third in the National League behind Pittsburgh's Honus Wagner's 126 RBI, and Philadelphia's Ed Delahanty, who had 108 RBI. Crawford's feat was even more impressive when you consider Cincinnati finished last giving him fewer opportunities to drive in runs during that 1901 season. Crawford was the American League's leader with 120 RBI in 1910 and 104 RBI in 1914. "Wahoo Sam" Crawford was elected to Baseball's Hall of Fame in 1956.

Publisher: Wolverine News Co., Detroit, MI * Manufacturer: Not Indicated * Type: Black & White * Postmark: Not Used * Value Index: B

SAM CRAWFORD, Bunting

HUGGINS
SECOND BASEMAN
PAR EXCELLENCE

While Miller Huggins is best remembered as Manager of the New York Yankees' outstanding teams during the 1920s, he was a fine second baseman for the Cincinnati Reds and St. Louis Cardinals. When a set of Postcards was issued in 1907 featuring various baseball scenes involving the Reds and their opponents, Miller Huggins was the only Cincinnati player featured in the set. He was probably selected because of his status as Cincinnati's leading batter, among starting players, with a .292 BA. Huggins was only 5-feet-6-inches tall, an excellent fielder with good range, and an astute student of the game. Consistency was his hallmark, as Huggins had a career .265 BA for 13 seasons in the Major Leagues. Huggins began his managerial career with the Cardinals in 1913 as player-manager and retired as an active player to devote full time to managing in 1917. He left St. Louis to become manager of the New York Yankees in 1918 and led them to their first American League Pennants beginning in 1921, 1922, and 1923. In 1921 and 1922 they lost to the New York Giants in the World Series and in 1923 they beat the Giants in the World Series. The Huggins' Yankees were World Champions again in 1927 and 1928, and he retired from the game in 1929 because of ill health. Miller Huggins became a member of the Baseball Hall of Fame for his outstanding success as a manager; however, his fine career as a player should not be overlooked.

Publisher: The Morgan Stationery Co., Cincinnati, OH * Manufacturer: Not Indicated * Type: Pre-Linen * Postmark: Not Used * Value Index: A

Publisher: H.M.Taylor, Detroit, MI * Manufacturer: Not Indicated * Type: Black & White * Postmark: Detroit, MI October 16, 1907 * Value Index: A

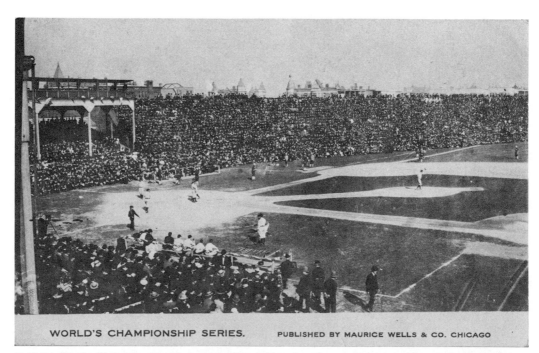

Publisher: Maurice Wells & Co. Chicago, IL * Manufacturer: Not Indicated * Type: Real Photograph * Postmark: Chicago, IL, October 18, 1907 * Value Index: A

Frank Chance's Cubs won four National League Pennants and two World Championships during his eight seasons as player-manager and was highly respected by opponents as well as his teammates. Chance's nickname was "Husk" because he was a husky 6 feet, 200 pounds. He was amazingly quick for his size and twice led the National League with 67 stolen bases in 1903 and 57 stolen bases in 1906, when the Cubs set the all-time record of 116 victories in a single season. Frank Chance exuded confidence as you can see by this photograph, taken during the 1907 World Series with the Detroit Tigers. Opposing manager Hughie Jennings and Tigers ace pitcher Wild Bill Donovan seem to be looking at Chance in awe. Note that Chance is wearing a matching diamond starburst ring and tie pin as he kibitzes on the Tigers bench before the game. The Cubs easily disposed of the Tigers in the Series winning four games to none, with the first game ending in a 3 to 3 tie. Because he crowded the plate when he batted, Chance was frequently hit by pitched balls to such a degree that he developed severe headaches from the "beanings" which ultimately required surgery. A native of Fresno, California Chance signed as a catcher with the Cubs in 1898 from the campus of Washington University in Irvington, California. Although Chance was a good catcher, he became an exceptional star when he converted to first base in 1902. Frank Chance's playing career ended with the New York Yankees in 1914 as he appeared in just one game. During 17 seasons he had a lifetime .291 BA. His clutch hitting and inspirational leadership made him one of the most respected players in Baseball history. The "Peerless Leader" was only 47 years old when he died in 1924 and he was elected to the Baseball Hall of Fame in 1946.

This interior view of West Side Park in Chicago shows a typical capacity crowd, there to see the Cubs host the American League Champion Detroit Tigers in the 1907 World Series. It was the second consecutive World Series for Frank Chance's Cubs and Chicago wanted to prove that they belonged among the great Baseball teams. The Cubs won 107 games in 1907, only nine less than their 116 victories during the prior year, with virtually the same team. Their famous "Stonewall Infield" was Baseball's best with the outfield of Frank Schulte, Jimmy Slagle, and Jimmy Sheckard more than adequate. Johnny Kling was an excellent Catcher and the pitching staff headed by Orvie Overall and Mordecai "Three Finger" Brown was superb. Overall led the National League with 23 victories and Brown had 19 wins. The other members of this magnificent pitching staff all had ERAs of less than two runs per game. Jack Pfiester was the National League's leader with a 1.15 ERA. Carl Lundgren was second with a 1.17 ERA, Brown was third with a 1.39 ERA, Ed Reulbach was fifth with a 1.69 ERA. Overall was sixth with a 1.70 ERA. These results show why the Cubs dominated the League 18 games in front of second place Pittsburgh. Cub pitchers ruled the 1907 World Series as they completely stymied Tiger batters in winning four games to none with one tie game. Ty Cobb had only 4 hits in 20 times at bat against the Cubs pitching, a mere .200 BA.

BROWN

Mordecai "Three Finger" Brown is an example of someone overcoming a great handicap and actually using it to his advantage in becoming one of baseball's all-time best pitchers. When Mordecai was seven years old, he was spending the summer on his Uncle David Beasley's farm. His hand was caught in a grinding machine necessitating the amputation of his right index finger and badly mangling his middle finger. Discussing the accident years later when Mordecai was the Chicago Cubs' star pitcher, David Beasley said, "It was a terrible thing at the time, but when he grew up the maimed hand enabled him to get unusual breaks on his pitches." Brown was an excellent pitcher and he beat the great New York Giants' pitcher Christy Mathewson nine straight times when they opposed each other on the mound. Brown was instrumental in leading the Cubs to the National League Pennant in 1906, 1907, 1908, and 1910, and he won 20 or more games during six consecutive years from 1906 to 1912. Perhaps his most memorable game occurred on Oct 8, 1908 in New York's Polo Grounds when the Cubs faced the Giants in a playoff for the National League Championship. Brown was under enormous pressure as he had received letters threatening his life. "I had a half-dozen 'Black Hand' letters in my coat pocket. We'll kill you if you pitch and beat the Giants." Brown did not start the game; however Jack Pfeister ran into difficulty in the first inning, as the Giants scored one run and had two runners on base with two out. Mordecai was summoned from the bullpen by Manager Frank Chance. He struck out the Giants' Art Devlin, ending the inning, and Chicago went on to beat Giants' ace Christy Mathewson by a 4 to 2 score. "I was about as good that day as I ever was in my life. That year, I had won 29 games, and what with relief work, had been in 43 winning ball games." Brown concluded his 14-year Major League career in 1916 with a total of 229 wins and only 131 losses.

Publisher: Novelty Cutlery Co., Canton, OH * Manufacturer: Not Indicated * Type: Black & White * Postmark: Not Used * Value Index: B

The Chicago Cubs and New York Giants were bitter rivals during the early 1900s and when they played each other capacity crowds would always attend. This interior view of West Side Park shows this usual "full house." In 1908 each game between the rivals was of vital importance, as the National League Pennant race went to the final game and finally to a play-off game. The dead ball was part of this era and the West Side Park was 340 feet long at the foul lines in right and left fields and 560 feet to center field. The dead ball and the long distances to the outfield seats helped to explain why the Cub HR leader, Joe Tinker, had only seven HR for the entire season and may have also been a factor in the closeness of the Pennant race.

Publisher: A.J. Schumann, Chicago, IL * Manufacturer: A.J. Schumann * Type: Real Photograph * Postmark: Not Used * Value Index: A

Fred Merkle, long-time first baseman with the New York Giants will live in infamy as the man who cost the Giants the 1908 National League Pennant. Merkle was never blamed by Manager John McGraw or his teammates. Despite a distinguished 16-year Major League career Merkle carried the nickname "Bonehead" to his grave. As the story is told, the Giants were playing their arch rivals, the Chicago Cubs. The score was tied with two out in the 9th inning. Harry McCormick was the base runner on third base and Merkle was the runner at first base. Al Bridwell singled sharply to center field scoring McCormick with what was thought to be the winning run. As was customary at the time, Merkle ran toward second

Publisher: Not Indicated * Manufacturer: Not Indicated * Type: Black & White * Postmark: Not Used * Value Index: A

base to show he could have reached the base, but before touching the bag, he turned and ran toward the clubhouse. Cub second baseman Johnny Evers retrieved the ball, raced to touch second base and then asked Chief Umpire Hank O'Day to declare Merkle out and to disallow the run. O'Day made no immediate decision and after conferring with National League President Harry Pulliam the next day, Merkle was ruled out. McCormick's winning run was not allowed, taking a victory away from the Giants that would have assured them of the National League Pennant. The two teams ended the regular season tied for first place necessitating a make-up game at the Polo Grounds on October 8. The Cubs won the game 4 to 2 and became National League Champions. This Postcard published in 1908 commemorated the historic event and shows Merkle as a hero in Chicago and a goat in New York.

This magnificent photograph showing the exterior of West Side Park, was taken during the early 1900s. The scene is the corner of Lincoln and Polk Streets. Lincoln Street is on the right parallel to the first base stands and Polk Street is on the left parallel to the third base seats. Note the horse-drawn carriage at the front of a line of automobiles parked on Lincoln Street. Only the wealthy could afford automobiles at that time. Notice the chauffeurs waiting to drive the automobile owners home after the game. All games were played during the daylight hours usually beginning at 3:00 PM and ending before 5:00 PM. The youngsters waiting outside the grandstands were hoping to catch a foul ball hit over the grandstand roof. It would be a

Publisher: A.J. Schumann, Chicago, IL * Manufacturer: A.J. Schumann * Type: Real Photograph * Postmark: Not Used * Value Index: A

souvenir of the game and, if returned to the Cubs' office, would enable them to gain free entry to the park.

Wild Bill Donovan enjoyed a great deal of success as a Major League pitcher. Extremely popular with teammates and fans alike, he enjoyed his most successful season when the Detroit Tigers won their first of three consecutive American League Pennants in 1907, compiling an astounding record of 26 wins and only 4 losses. Donovan's winning percentage of .867 was the best in the League. Like many fastball pitchers, he often had control problems. For example, in 1901, pitching with the Brooklyn Dodgers the righthander led the National League with 152 walks and 226 strikeouts. In 1909, at the peak of his career, Donovan suffered an injury to his pitching arm and, although he came back to win 17 games in 1910, he was not the same pitcher after the injury. Donovan won just one game in 1912 with the Tigers and was out of Baseball for three seasons, until 1915 when he joined the New York Highlanders. Wild Bill came back with the Tigers in 1918 for one more attempt at pitching and won only one game. His career totals are impressive with 188 wins and 137 losses compiled over 18 Major League seasons. This photograph shows Donovan at the water cooler in the Detroit dugout in 1907, the year he had the distinction of being the best pitcher in Baseball.

Publisher: Wolverine News Co., Detroit, MI * Manufacturer: Not Indicated * Type: Black & White * Postmark: Not Used * Value Index: B

"WILD BILL" at the Water Wagon

WORLD'S SERIES SOUVENIR

TWO
OF A
KIND

COPYRIGHT 1909
BY W. W. SMITH

COBB

DAVIS & MASON, PITTSBURGH

WAGNER

Publisher: W.W. Smith, Pittsburgh, PA * Manufacturer: Davis & Mason, Pittsburgh, PA * Type: Black & White * Postmark: Pittsburgh, PA, October 8, 1909 * Value Index: A

Unquestionably the most famous players of their day were Detroit Tigers' star outfielder Ty Cobb and Pittsburgh Pirates' great shortstop Honus Wagner. When Detroit and Pittsburgh met in the 1909 World Series Baseball fans argued as to who was the better player. The publisher of this Postcard gave each player equal billing; however, note that Wagner's picture is larger than Cobb's picture. One could say they were clairvoyant as the Pirates won the World Series four games to three and Wagner had a .333 BA compared to a .231 BA for Cobb. Cobb was 22 years old while Wagner was 35 years old and had more experience. Cobb had a lifetime .367 BA in 22 seasons and Wagner a .327 BA in 21 seasons. Both men were exceptionally fast and outstanding base runners who led their leagues numerous times in stolen bases. Baseball historians continue to debate over the merits of each player. In the final analysis, the title on this Postcard is correct in stating they were "Two of a Kind"... both great.

When Connie Mack and Ben Shibe built Columbia Park in 1901 they realized it was a temporary structure. As the Philadelphia Athletics had greater success they required a more modern facility. In 1908, when the information became known that a new facility was planned, Postcard publisher Frank H. Taylor became active by publishing Postcards showing the park approximately one year before its opening. Taylor's Postcards are considered very rare and desirable among collectors. The Postcards published in 1908 and 1909 are distinguishable by the information on the them. For the Postcards published in 1908 :" The greatest ball park in the world, 21st Street and Lehigh Avenue. Philadelphia. Seating Capacity 23,000. Steel and Concrete construction. Will open for season of 1909."

Shibe Park, Athletic Base Ball Club, American League, 21st Street and Lehigh Avenue, Philadelphia. The Largest and Best Appointed Base Ball Park in the World.

Publisher: Frank H. Taylor, Philadelphia, PA * Manufacturer: Not Indicated * Type: Pre-Linen * Postmark: Pittsburgh, PA, October 8, 1909 * Value Index: A

For the Postcards published in 1909:

"Shibe Park Athletic Baseball Club American League. 21st Street and Lehigh Avenue. Philadelphia. The largest and best appointed baseball park in the world."

In keeping with these lofty sounding accolades, Shibe Park was as good as advertised. The photograph shown above is Shibe Park upon its completion.

Washington Park in Brooklyn was the home of the Brooklyn Dodgers from April 15, 1898 until they moved into the new Ebbets Field in 1913. Washington Park continued as a Major League Baseball facility when the Federal League came into existence in 1914. The park was completely rebuilt by the bakery magnates Robert and George Ward, who owned the Brooklyn Federal League team known as the "Tip Tops." There were approximately 15,000 fans at the opening on May 11, 1914. When the Federal League ended after the 1915 season, the Washington Park activities also ceased. As with most wooden-stand ball parks the facility became expendable with the beginning of the era of modern steel and concrete stadiums. This photograph taken in 1909, shows an overflow crowd of 23,000 fans at Washington Park watching the Dodgers in action.

Brooklyn Base Ball Park, 1909.

Publisher: Pictorial News Co., New York, NY, Card No. 63012 * Manufacturer: Not Indicated * Type: Pre-Linen * Postmark: Pittsburgh, PA, September 7, 1910 * Value Index: A

When Denton True Young joined the Cleveland Spiders of the National League in 1890, the six-foot-two-inch righthander had already earned his nickname "Cy" short for Cyclone, a tribute to his fast ball. Young was given the name by Canton, Ohio sportswriters when he pitched for Canton in the Tri-State League in 1888. When Cy Young's 22-year Major League career ended, he had compiled 509 career victories, a record that will probably never be broken. In 1908, Young won 21 games for the Boston Red Sox although he was 41 years old at the time. Young participated in the first modern World Series in 1903, winning two games and leading Boston of the American League to a stunning upset over the Pittsburgh Pirates of the established National League. The American League had been founded in 1901 and was only two years old when the Puritans (Red Sox) met the Pirates. Most people thought they would not have a chance to win the World Series. Having a pitcher of Cy Young's magnitude on your side made up for lots of deficiencies. As examples, he pitched three no hitters and won 20 or more games in one season during 16 years, including 14 years in a row. He is immortalized by the Cy Young Award, given annually to the outstanding pitcher in both the American and National Leagues. Also, Young accomplished his great pitching feat of 509 wins under less than perfect conditions. As he said years after his career was over, "There were disadvantages playing back then including poor fields, poorer equipment, bad food, lousy traveling conditions, no showers, sooty trains, and noisy rooming houses so full of bed bugs, they'd keep you up all night."

Publisher: A.C. Williams, Boston, MA * Manufacturer: Not Indicated * Type: Black & White * Postmark: Unionville, MD March 29, 1912 * Value Index: A

Delivering the Goods.

H.M. Rose was a Baseball fan and Postcard publisher who devoted much time and effort in producing Postcards of interest to Baseball fans. In 1907 he issued a set of 156 Major and Minor League player Postcards that are highly prized and sought after today as collector's items. He was extremely proud of the fact that Philadelphia was the first to build a modern steel and concrete ball park and provided a Postcard as soon as the park was ready. The process of embossing was used to raise a portion of the Postcard surface producing a three-dimensional effect. The H.M. Rose Postcards, are among the rarest items at this date and have been regarded as a legacy for excellence.

COPYRIGHT 1909 BY H. M. ROSE

Greetings from Philadelphia

SHIBE PARK

Publisher: H.M. Rose, Philadelphia, PA * Manufacturer: Not Indicated * Type: Pre-Linen * Postmark: Not Used * Value Index: A

This interior photograph of Shibe Park was taken in 1909 when it opened as the first modern steel and concrete stadium. The stands extending along the left field foul line were uncovered. A roof was added in 1913 and additional stands were erected in left field. The original dimensions were 360 feet along the right and left foul lines, 393 feet in the power alleys of right and left center field, and 515 feet to center field. The opening day on April 12, 1909 was a major event. Among the Baseball dignitaries in attendance was George Wright, star shortstop of the first professional team, the Cincinnati Red Stockings of 1869. Overwhelmed when he saw the new stadium with an overflow crowd of 30,162 fans he said, "It is the most

Shibe Park Baseball Grounds, Philadelphia, Pa.

Publisher: M.L. Metrochrom * Manufacturer: M.L. Metrochrom * Type: Pre-Linen * Postmark: Not Used * Value Index: C

remarkable sight I have ever witnessed." Wright was one of Baseball's pioneers who helped to spread professional Baseball throughout America. He did not dream of the popularity that the game would achieve. The Athletics had 674,913 spectators at Shibe Park during that year, a record that would not be broken by them until 1925.

During the winter of 1908-1909, Pittsburgh Pirates' owner Barney Dreyfuss realized that antiquated Exposition Park had outlived its usefulness. It had been their home since 1891. Dreyfuss knew the Philadelphia Athletics were planning Shibe Park as a modern facility. He formulated his plans quickly and asked his friend, the steel magnate Andrew Carnegie, to help negotiate for some property in the Schenley Park section of the city. Years later Dreyfuss recalled, "There was nothing there but a livery stable and a hot house and a few cows grazing over the countryside." This Postcard, featuring an artist's sketch, was available while the park was being built. The new ball park was described in the 1910 edition *Reach Guide*. "Words also must fail to picture in the mind's

New Base Ball Stadium and Park, "Forbes Field," Pittsburg, Pa.

Publisher: The Acmegraph Co., Chicago, IL * Manufacturer: The Acmegraph Co. * Type: Pre-Linen * Postmark: Not Used * Value Index: C

eye adequately the splendors of the magnificent pile President Dreyfuss erected as a tribute to the national game, a beneficence to Pittsburgh and an enduring monument to himself."

June 30, 1909 was an important day in the sports history of Pittsburgh, as the Pirates had a record crowd of 30,338 fans in their new Forbes Field. The ground breaking for the $2,000,000 facility was begun on March 1, 1909, and this opening game was approximately four months later. The new stadium was more than twice the size of Exposition Park which had been the Pirates' home since 1891. This photograph was taken from center field looking toward the main doubledecked grandstand filled with standing-room-only fans. The right field and left field foul lines were 372 feet and 360 feet respectively and the center field flagpole was 462 feet from home plate. During this time period the dead ball was used and HRs were not as important to the game. During the first

Publisher: The Union News Company, New York, NY, Card No. 684 * Manufacturer: Chatauqua Photographic Co., Pittsburgh, PA * Type: Pre-Linen * Postmark: Not Used * Value Index: B

season, center fielder Tommy Leach led the Pirates with 6 HRs and shortstop Honus Wagner had 5 HRs and led the team with 100 RBI.

Albert Goodwill Spalding was one of Baseball's pioneers. He was a star pitcher and outstanding manager in the first professional league, the National Association. He won 207 and lost 56 games during the five years that the National Association was in existence, playing with the Boston Red Stockings. Gambling and rowdyism were rampant in the National Association and Spalding led a group which formed a new league that was free of these problems. In 1876 the National League was formed with Spalding as pitcher and manager of the Chicago White Stockings. He won 46 and lost 12 games in leading the White Stockings to the first Pennant in the League. He was also a businessman and he understood the

POLO GROUNDS, 157th STREET AND EIGHTH AVENUE
Can be reached by Sixth and Ninth Avenue Elevated direct to the grounds, and Broadway Subway, stopping at 155th St., and a short walk to the grounds. Seating capacity estimated at 40,000. Reserved Seats as well as Box Seats on sale by A. G. Spalding & Bros., No. 126 Nassau St. and No. 29 W. 42nd St.

Publisher: A.G. Spalding & Bros., New York, NY * Manufacturer: Not Indicated * Type: Pre-Linen * Postmark: Not Used * Value Index: A

importance of Baseball. He began a chain of sporting goods stores throughout the country called A.G. Spalding & Brothers. He also sold tickets for the games in the major cities. This rare Postcard, showing the Polo Grounds in New York City, indicates that tickets for games could be purchased at his stores. "Polo Grounds, 157th Street and Eighth Avenue. Can be reached by 6th and 9th Avenue Elevated direct to the grounds. Seating capacity estimated at 40,000. Reserve seats as well as Box Seats on sale by A.G. Spalding and Bros., No. 126 Nassau St. and No. 29 W. 42nd St." This Postcard was issued in 1908 or 1909 when the stadium at the Polo Grounds was basically a wooden structure.

Another of the rare Spalding advertising Postcards distributed by A.G. Spalding & Brothers in 1909 at their Chicago store, showing a panoramic view of West Side Park. The 1909 text, "Beautiful West Side Baseball Park. The Chicago Playing Home of the world-renowned "Cubs." This has been the scene of the most historic diamond battles during the past decade that this country has known. On Sept. 16th last this park was visited by President Taft and many notable citizens whose names are household words throughout the country. The "Cubs" constitute one of the greatest modern machines of baseball, and in addition to twice winning the world's championship, they have broken records almost without number. The manager of the

BEAUTIFUL WEST SIDE BASEBALL PARK
The Chicago playing home of the world-renowned "Cubs." This has been the scene of some of the most historic diamond battles during the past decade that this country has known. On Sept. 16th last this park was visited by President Taft and many notable citizens, whose names are household words throughout the country. The "Cubs" constitute one of the greatest modern machines of baseball, and in addition to twice winning the world's championship, they have broken records almost without number. The manager of the team, Frank L. Chance, who is known as the "Peerless Leader," is one of the foremost characters in the game. Tickets for these games are sold at A. G. Spalding & Bros.' store, 147 Wabash Avenue, daily from 9 a. m. until 1 p. m. Seats can be reserved by mail, telephone or telegraph.

Publisher: A.G. Spalding & Bros., Chicago, IL * Manufacturer: Not Indicated * Type: Pre-Linen * Postmark: Not Used * Value Index: A

team, Frank L. Chance, who is known as the "Peerless Leader" is one of the foremost characters in the game. Tickets for these games are sold at A.G. Spalding and Bros' store, 147 Wabash Avenue. Daily from 9 AM until 1 PM. Seats can be reserved by mail, telephone or telegraph."

Advertisers have always used Baseball as a promotional vehicle and when the Samuel H. French & Co. did all of the masonry work at Shibe Park in Philadelphia they were justifiably proud of the magnificent job. This Postcard was issued immediately after the park opened in 1909 and states:

"Shibe Ball Park is the home of the White Elephants. It was opened in 1909 and is considered the handsomest ball park in America. 4000 barrels of Dexter Portland Cement used in its construction. Sole Agents. Samuel H. French & Co. Established 1844. Philadelphia."

Shibe Park and Forbes Field in Pittsburgh both opened during the 1909 season and were the first of the modern steel and

SHIBE BALL PARK. Another reminder of our "Athletic" advertisement department. Samuel H. French & Co. (9)

Publisher: Samuel H. French & Co., Philadelphia, PA, Card No. 9 * Manufacturer: Not Indicated * Type: Pre-Linen * Postmark: Philadelphia, PA, September 7, 1911 * Value Index: B

concrete ball parks. Baseball fans, accustomed to the wooden structures, marveled at how beautiful they were. Shibe Park was in use for more than 60 years. After the Athletics left Philadelphia for Kansas City at the end of the 1954 season the National League Phillies purchased Shibe Park and used it until 1970 when Veterans Stadium was built.

Robert Alexander "Bob" Unglaub had an undistinguished six-year Major League career. In 1909 he led the last-place Washington Senators with 41 RBI. The photograph used on this Postcard is the only known view of the American League park. The Senators in that year won 42 and lost 110 games. They were 56 games behind the Detroit Tigers and 20 games behind the seventh-place St Louis team. Unglaub showed his versatility during that season by playing first base, outfield, second base, and third base. He also led the Senators with three HRs. His final season with the Senators was 1910 and he had 44 RBI with a .234 BA. He had a career .258 BA during six major league seasons.

Publisher: Barr-Farnham Co., Washington, DC * Manufacturer: Barr-Farnham Co. * Type: Real Photograph * Postmark: Not Used * Value Index: A

Publisher: A.C. Dietsche Co., Detroit, MI * Manufacturer: A.C. Dietsche Co. * Type: Black-White * Value Index: A

The 1909 Detroit Tigers shown in Bennett Park won the American League Pennant for the third consecutive year. A record of 98 wins and 54 defeats enabled them to finish the season 3-1/2 games ahead of the Philadelphia Athletics. Ty Cobb, seated on the far left side in the second row, won the Triple Crown in 1909. Other important players included Hall-of-Fame outfielder Sam Crawford who had a 314 BA and 97 RBIs. The pitching staff was led by righthander George Mullin with 29 wins and 9 losses. Others included righthanders Ed Willett with 21 victories and Ed Summers with 19 wins. Their opponents in the 1909 World Series were the Pittsburgh Pirates. Despite a great effort, the Tigers lost the Series four games to three.

John McGraw is considered one of the best managers in Baseball history. Al. Bridwell, who was the New York Giants' shortstop for 3-1/2 seasons under McGraw, spoke of his manager, "The reason McGraw was a great manager—and he was the greatest—was because he knew how to handle men. Some of the players he rode and others he didn't. In knowing each player and how to handle him, nobody came anywhere close to McGraw." During the 30 years from 1902 to 1932, McGraw known as "The Little Napoleon" because of his skill as a tactician, won 10 National League Pennants. He had the ability to assess the proper skills and made stars of players who

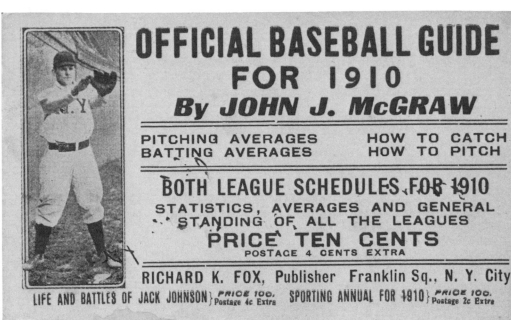

Publisher: Richard K. Fox, New York, NY * Manufacturer: Not Indicated * Type: U.S. Government Postal Card * Postmark: New York, NY, May 10, 1910 * Value Index: A

others thought did not have Baseball talent. McGraw began as a Major League player with the Baltimore Orioles in 1891. Only 5 feet-7 inches tall and weighing 150 pounds, he was a tough competitor, and an instant crowd pleaser. If he had not become a manager then he would have become a member of the Hall of Fame with a career .334 BA compiled over 16 seasons. McGraw was primarily a third baseman and an innovator developing tactics such as the hit and run. McGraw's name was sought after for many products including the 1910 Baseball Guide illustrated on this promotional Postcard.

Although the new League Park in Cleveland did not open until 1910, the design of the new stadium was known in advance and was used in 1909 by A.G. Spalding to promote the sale of tickets. The text on the Postcard is: "How the New Cleveland Grandstand will look, Details: Length of grandstand, 503 feet; length of pavilion, 423 feet; distance from home plate to grand stand, 76 feet; home plate to right field fence on the foul line, 280 feet; home plate to left field fence on the foul line, 385 feet. Seating capacity: 260 front box seats, $1.25; 340 rear box seats, $1.00; 2,400 reserved seats, $1.00; 7,700 grand stand seats 75 cents; 6,500 pavilion seats, 50 cents; 2,000 bleacher seats, 25 cents; total seats 19,200. Made of steel and concrete. A. G. Spalding & Bros., 741 Euclid Ave."

HOW THE NEW CLEVELAND GRAND STAND WILL LOOK

DETAILS:—Length of grand stand, 503 feet; length of pavillion, 423 feet; distance from home plate to grand stand, 76 feet; distance from first base to grand stand, 78 feet; distance from third base to grand stand, 70 feet; home plate to right field fence on foul line, 290 feet; home plate to left field fence on foul line, 385 feet. Seating capacity: 260 front box seats, $1.25; 340 rear box seats, $1.00; 2,400 reserved seats, $1.00; 7,700 grand stand seats, 75 cents; 6,500 pavilion seats, 50 cents; 2,000 bleacher seats, 25 cents; total seats, 19,200. Made of steel and concrete.

A. G. SPALDING & BROS., 741 EUCLID AVE.

Publisher: A.G. Spalding & Bros., Cleveland, OH, Card No. 613 * Manufacturer: Not Indicated * Type: Pre-Linen * Postmark: Cleveland, Ohio, May 11, 1910 * Value Index: A

This exterior photograph of the new League Park taken during the initial season of 1910 shows how accessible it was to public transportation. Trolley tracks are clearly visible on all sides of the Stadium located at East 66th Street and Lexington Avenue. When the original wooden League Park was built for the National League Spiders in 1891, the team owner was trolley magnate Frank Robison. He selected this particular site because his trolley line ran directly to it. Trolleys were the principal means of transportation and it was imperative that ball parks were located within easy reach of the general public. Note the 25-foot screen above the 20-foot wall in right field shown on the right-hand side of the illustration. Babe

Publisher: The Cleveland News Co., Cleveland, OH, Card No. M3347 Manufacturer: Americhrom, New York, NY * Type: Pre-Linen * Postmark: Cleveland, OH, November 20, 1910 * Value Index: C

Ruth hit his 500th career HR out of this ball park. A Cleveland youngster named Jack Geiser retrieved the ball outside the stadium and returned it to Babe Ruth. The grateful Ruth gave Geiser a $20.00 bill, an autographed baseball, and an opportunity to sit in the Yankee Dugout.

After the opening of the first two modern Baseball stadiums, Shibe Park in Philadelphia and Forbes Field in Pittsburgh, new stadiums were constructed all over the United States. Comiskey Park opened in Chicago and New League Park in Cleveland during 1910; New Polo Grounds in New York, 1911; Navin Field in Detroit and Fenway Park in Boston, 1912; Ebbets Field in Brooklyn, 1913; Weegham Park, Federal League, in Chicago, 1914; and Braves Field in Boston, 1915. When Chicago became a charter member of the American League in 1901, Charles Comiskey leased the South End Grounds, which had been the home of the Chicago Wanderers Cricket Club. With a seating capacity of only 7,500 he began looking for a new stadium in

Publisher: Empire Art Co., Chicago, IL, Card No. 78R-28993 * Manufacturer: Not Indicated * Type: Pre-Linen * Postmark: Des Moines, IA, September 23, 1912 * Value Index: B

1903. In 1909 he hired Zachary Taylor Davis to design his special stadium and it exceeded all expectations. Comiskey was so proud of Comiskey Park that he referred to it as "The Baseball Palace of the World." When it opened on July 1, 1910, 28,000 fans were crowded into every possible space to watch the White Sox lose to the St. Louis Browns by a 2 to 0 score. With the strength of the Sox in pitching, Comiskey wanted a spacious ball park. The original dimensions were 363 feet for the left and right field foul lines and 420 feet to dead center field. Comiskey Park, at 35th Street and Shields Avenue was used by the Sox from 1910 through 1990. The Sox moved into their new stadium across the street in 1991.

This photograph was taken on April 22, 1910 with the grand opening of Cleveland's new steel and concrete League Park. The Cleveland fans had a replacement for the decaying wooden League Park in use since 1891. The new park was built on the same site at Lexington Avenue and East 66th Street with all of the modern conveniences and space for approximately 27,000 fans. The wall extending from right field to the bleachers in left and center fields was only 290 feet from home plate giving left-handed batters an advantage. When there were overflow crowds the right field area was roped off to accommodate more fans and the distance was only 240 feet from home plate. There was a 25-foot-high screen above the 20-foot wall, however, that

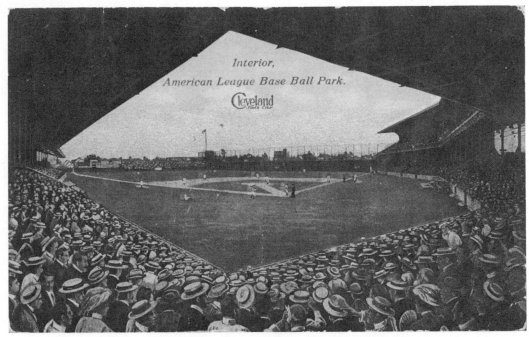

Publisher: Century Postcard Co., Cleveland, OH, Card No. 18600, * Type: Pre-Linen * Postmark: Eagleville, Ohio, September 25, 1914 * Value Index: B

did not keep the batters from hitting the ball out of the park. Babe Ruth of the New York Yankees hit his 500th HR over the right field screen in 1929. During their first season in the new League Park, the Indians finished in fifth place and, except for special days such as the opening game against Detroit on April 22, they failed to attract large crowds. After 1946, the Indians used Municipal Stadium.

The Philadelphia Athletics had almost instant success at Shibe Park. Although manager Connie Mack's team finished second to the Detroit Tigers in 1909, they won the American League Pennant in 1910 and 1911. They added to their glory by winning the world championship in both years. In 1910, they beat the Chicago Cubs four games to one in the World Series. The Athletics were basically the same team in 1910 and 1911. Harry Davis was the captain and first baseman. The future Hall-of-Famers Eddie Collins and Frank Baker were at second and third base. Jack Barry was the shortstop. Danny Murphy, Rube Oldring, Topsy Hartsell, and Bristol Lord patrolled the outfield while Ira Thomas and Jack Lapp shared the catching duties. The magnificent pitching staff was anchored by

Publisher: W.N. Jennings, Philadelphia, PA * Manufacturer: Not Indicated * Type: Pre-Linen * Postmark: Altoona, PA, January 3, 1912 * Value Index B

future Hall-of-Famer Jack Coombs who led the American League with 30 victories in 1910 and 29 victories in 1911. Shibe Park was only three years old in 1911.

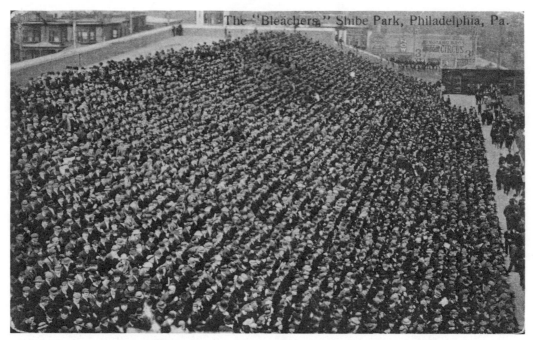

Publisher: P. Sander, Philadelphia, PA * Manufacturer: Not Indicated * Type: Sepia & White * Postmark: Not Used * Value Index A

These two photographs appear to be identical, although one is designated Bleachers Shibe Park and the other is designated Bleachers New York. The photograph was taken at Shibe Park and used for both scenes. The publisher decided to use one photograph for both Postcards rather than take a second photograph. He did distinguish between the two by coloring Shibe Park in sepia and coloring the New York bleachers in blue. He was not completely wrong as the bleachers generally look the same wherever they are located. They usually contain bench-type seats as opposed to the more expensive chairback seats. The name bleachers came from the wood being bleached by the sun. Bleacher sections were always uncovered with the exception of Tiger Stadium in Detroit. Chicago sports writer Hugh Fullerton gave bleacher fans an added status when he wrote in 1912, "The Bleacherites usually are much better posted on the game than those patrons who occupy the grandstand boxes and seats and are much more dreaded by the players because of their caustic criticism."

Publisher: P. Sander, New York, NY * Manufacturer: Not Indicated * Type: Blue & White * Postmark: Not Used * Value Index: A

The 1910 Philadelphia Athletics had a fine blend of pitching, defense, and hitting to win the American League Pennant by 14-1/2 games over the second place New York Highlanders. Jack Coombs won 30 and lost 9 games to lead a pitching staff with two other future Hall-of-Famers: Chief Bender won 22 and lost 5 games and Eddie Plank won 17 and lost 10 games. The infield included Captain Harry Davis at first base, Eddie Collins at second base, Jack Barry at shortstop, and Frank "Home Run" Baker at third base. Collins and Baker also entered the Hall of Fame. When the Athletics entered the American League in 1901 someone commented "There is not enough room for two teams in Philadelphia. The

Publisher: Not Indicated * Manufacturer: Not Indicated * Type: Black & White * Postmark: Philadelphia, PA, September 9, 1910 * Value Index: A

Athletics will be a white elephant." Co-Owner and Manager Connie Mack adapted the white elephant as his team symbol and it remains today.

When Connie Mack was creating his first American League Team in Philadelphia he searched for quality players. In his book, *MY 66 YEARS IN THE BIG LEAGUES* he said, "I found a boy wonder at Gettysburg College who looked like a comer to me. His name was Eddie Plank." The boy wonder left Gettysburg College to become a Hall of Fame pitcher without spending one day in the minor leagues. During his first season with the Athletics, the 5-foot-11-1/2-inch lefthander won 17 and lost 13 games. When Plank's Major League career ended 17 years later, in 1917, with the St. Louis Browns he had won 325 and lost 190 games. When Philadelphia won its first Pennant in 1902 Plank was a 20-game winner, the first of eight 20-game years. His best year was in 1905 when he won 26 and lost 12 games. He pitched superbly in the 1905 World Series against the New York Giants but lost to Christy Mathewson by a score of 3 to 0 and then lost a 1 to 0 heartbreaker to Joe McGinnity, as the one Giants' run scored on two Philadelphia errors. Plank had some revenge when the Athletics won four games to two in the 1913 World Series against the Giants. Plank won the final game 3 to 1 against Mathewson.

Publisher: Monarch Typewriter Co., Philadelphia, PA * Manufacturer: Not Indicated * Type: Sepia & White * Postmark: Not Used * Value Index: A

EDWARD S. PLANK, Pitcher

Publisher: Elite Postcard Shop, Washington, DC, Card No. 1 * Manufacturer: Elite Postcard Shop * Type: Real Photograph *
Postmark: Not Used * Value Index: A

On March 17, 1911, the Washington Senators received terrible news while they were in spring training in Atlanta. Their ball park located on 7th Street and Florida Avenue had been destroyed by fire. A plumber doing some work with an acetylene torch had accidentally set fire to the wooden structure. President Tom Noyes, although badly shaken by the news, said he would have a new park ready for opening day on April 12 against the Boston Red Sox. The Elite Postcard Shop began to document the construction of the new park. They produced a series of photographs for Postcards on April 1, only 11 days before the completion of the work. The upper Postcard (No. 1) shows the wooden support beams for the rows of seats being put in place by the construction workers. The lower Postcard (No. 5) was taken later in the day and indicates the remaining work to be done. Note the bags of cement in the middle of the photograph waiting to be mixed and poured as the construction workers prepare the wooden support beams for the grandstand.

Publisher: Elite Postcard Shop, Washington, DC, Card No. 5 * Manufacturer: Elite Postcard Shop * Type: Real Photograph *
Postmark: Not Used * Value Index: A

Publisher: Elite Postcard Shop, Washington, DC, Card No. 6 * Manufacturer: Elite Postcard Shop * Type: Real Photograph *
Postmark: Not Used * Value Index: A

Five days later, on April 6, the upper photograph (No. 6) shows the concrete has been poured in specific areas of the Ball Park and workers continue to build support beams in other sections. The lower photograph (No. 18) was taken on April 10 and shows seats being installed. These extremely rare Postcards are part of a larger set because the new park was photographed until completion and through opening day. Washington Post sports editor Joe Jackson provided the color for this memorable event. "As 16,000 exuberant 33rd degree fans rose with the incoherent babble of sound that is the cry of the rooter, President William Howard Taft posed for a moment, swung his arm, and hurled the ball straight and true to Dolly Gray, the Washington pitcher." President Taft, an avid Baseball fan, began the tradition of throwing out the ceremonial first ball in 1910. This tradition has continued with each President through Richard Nixon participating in at least one season opening game until Washington lost its Major League franchise in 1971.

Publisher: Elite Postcard Shop, Washington, DC, Card No. 18 * Manufacturer: Elite Postcard Shop * Type: Real
Photograph * Postmark: Not Used * Value Index: A

First baseman Harry Davis was a favorite of Connie Mack. When Mack was forming his team for the 1901 season, Harry was one of the first players selected and he also became team captain. The Athletics won American League Championships in 1902, 1905, 1910, and 1911. When Davis's career was ending in 1911, Connie Mack decided to honor his star with a special day at Shibe Park. The Postcard in this illustration has the following message on the back side: "Dear Friend: Reserve Wednesday, May 31st, and have your friends do the same. We want every fan in Philadelphia to be at Shibe Park on this day, so we can show our appreciation of what Captain Davis has done for Baseball and the city of his birth. Mail this card to a friend as a reminder, Sincerely Yours, Connie Mack." Harry was 5 feet-10 inches tall and had played baseball at Girard College. In the era of the dead ball he won the HR championship in 1904 with 10 HRs in 1905 with 8 HRs in 1906 with 12 HRs, and in 1907 with 8 HRs. He led the League with 83 RBI in 1905 and 96 RBI in 1906. He stayed with Mack as player-coach through 1917. He had a lifetime .277 BA.

HARRY DAVIS DAY
SHIBE PARK
WEDNESDAY, MAY 31st

Publisher: Philadelphia Athletics * Manufacturer: Not Indicated * Type: Black & White *
Postmark: Not Used: Value Index: A

This artist's rendering shows the Polo Grounds after it reopened on June 28, 1911. A fire earlier in the season destroyed the old wooden grandstand and all the seats except for the bleachers in center field. Note how well the people dressed to attend a game. Giants owner John T. Brush did not spare any expense in creating an ultimate stadium. The new ball park was officially designated Brush Stadium; however, the fans continued to use the name Polo Grounds. The upper right-hand corner has a cameo portrait of manager John McGraw. He came to the Giants as a manager in 1902, although he played in a few games until 1906. Brush Stadium, or Polo Grounds, could only seat 16,000 spectators when it opened and work continued on it throughout the season. Eventually the seating was expanded to 34,000, in time for the World Series against the Philadelphia Athletics.

Publisher: Success Postal Card Co., New York, NY, Card No. 1148 * Manufacturer: Not Indicated * Type: Pre-Linen *
Postmark: New York, NY, October 6, 1914 * Value Index: C

Righthander Addie Joss of the Cleveland Naps had a fabulous career, although only nine years in length.

He won 160 and lost 97 games before he passed away from tubercular meningitis in 1911. Joss joined the team in 1902 and was an immediate favorite with fans. He was tall, handsome, and well-educated. Joss was a 17-game winner during his first year in the Major Leagues. On October 2, 1908 he outdueled Chicago's Big Ed Walsh by a 1 to 0 score, pitching a perfect game by retiring all 27 batters. He accomplished this feat during a 24-victory season. In 1907 he led the American League with 27 wins. Everything seemed to be going well for Joss when the disease struck him. His record slipped to 13 wins and 14 losses in 1909 and 5 wins and 5 losses in 1910, although one of those wins was a no-hitter.

Publisher: Not Indicated * Manufacturer: Not Indicated * Type: Real Photograph * Postmark: Not Used * Value Index: A

To raise money for his wife and son, an All Star Game was held on July 11 at League Park. A Cleveland newspaper described it, "The greatest array of players ever seen on one field." In this illustrious group you can see Ty Cobb, Eddie Collins, Sam Crawford, Frank "Home Run" Baker, Tris Speaker, Walter Johnson, and Napoleon Lajoie, all destined for the Hall of Fame. Note the Tiger star Ty Cobb, second from the right, is wearing a Cleveland uniform. Perhaps he forgot to bring his uniform to the game. The All Stars defeated the Naps by a 5 to 3 score with more than $13,000 raised for the Joss family.

Loyalty and hard work produced results for Frank Navin, president of the Detroit Tigers from 1908 to his death in 1935. In 1904 Navin was the business manager and small stockholder in the Ball Club. Tiger owner William Yawkee promised his enthusiastic young secretary that if the Tigers won a Pennant he would make him one-half owner; Navin became one-half owner in 1907. Bennett Park had been the Tiger home since 1901 and had space for only 8,500 spectators. In order to provide for the fans who wished to see Ty Cobb in action the park was expanded to seat 23,000 people and the playing field was turned 90 degrees. The newly named Navin Field opened on April 20, 1912. Navin Field was expanded in 1924 when the stands along the first and third base lines were double-decked to create space for 29,000 fans.

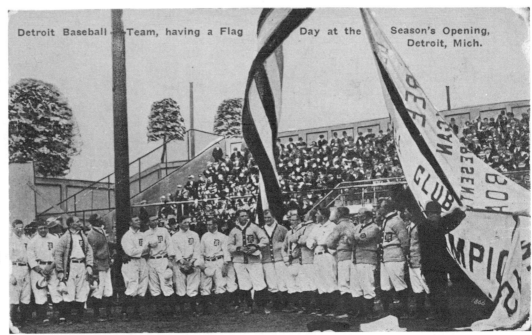

Publisher: United News Co., Detroit MI, Card No. 1866 * Manufacturer: Not Indicated * Type: Pre-Linen * Postmark: Detroit, MI, February 19, 1915 * Value Index: B

Redland Field in Cincinnati was built of necessity. Fire destroyed a major portion of the Palace of the Fans in the Fall of 1911 and the wooden structure had to be replaced for the 1912 season. The decision was made to build a modern stadium of steel and concrete. Redland Field was rebuilt on the same site and opened on April 11, 1912 with the formal dedication on May 18, 1912. Among the celebrities at the dedication were Ban Johnson, former Cincinnati sports writer and then president of the American League and Charles A. Comiskey, owner of the Chicago White Sox who had managed the Reds in 1890. Among the features in Redland Field that pleased all the players were clubhouse facilities for the home and visiting teams. Redland Field had

Cincinnati Base Ball Park, Cincinnati, O.
(C) Young & Carl, Cincinnati

Publisher: Young & Carl, Cincinnati, OH, Card No. 2261 * Manufacturer: Superior Postcard Co., Cincinnati, OH * Type: Pre-Linen * Postmark: Cincinnati, OH, July 25, 1913 * Value Index: C

large open spaces in the outfield. The right and left foul lines were 360 feet from home plate and it was 420 feet to centerfield. In their first season at the new home the Reds finished fourth in the National League and center fielder Armando Karsans from Cuba was the club's only .300 hitter with a .312 BA.

Hilltop Park was home to the New York Highlanders from 1903 to 1912. This view from the third base seats shows the wooden grandstand and the bleacher seats which extend along the right field foul line. The outfield was 365 feet along the left field line, 542 feet to center field, and 400 feet along the right field line. The pitchers enjoyed much success at this spacious park. Walter Johnson of the Washington Senators pitched three consecutive shutouts at Hilltop Park during four days in 1908. In 1912 the owners Frank Farrell and Bill Devery accepted an offer to use the more modern facilities at the Polo Grounds until the completion of Yankee Stadium.

American League Base Ball Park, New York, N.Y.

Publisher: Not Indicated, Card No. 25893 * Manufacturer: Not Indicated * Type: Pre-Linen * Postmark: Grand Central Station, NY, April 23, 1912 * Value Index: B

This photograph of Fenway Park shows the stadium when it opened in 1912. Its capacity for 35,000 fans is the same today. The policeman on horseback was a deterrent against any potential problems. During the 1912 season Manager Jake Stahl was leading the Red Sox to 105 victories with a 14-game lead over second-place Washington. The Washington team was managed for the first time by Clark Griffith who later owned the Senators. Centerfielder Tris Speaker led the Red Sox with a .384 BA and Smokey Joe Wood was compiling an unbelievable record of 34 wins and 5 losses. The Red Sox extended their winning season to the World Series, beating the Giants four games to three. The Boston fans considered the opening of the park as a good omen and the Red Sox were dominant in the American League for the remainder of the decade.

Publisher: Not Indicated, Card No. 861 * Manufacturer: Not Indicated * Type: Pre-Linen * Postmark: Not Used * Value Index: A

If Harry Frazee, the Broadway theatrical producer and owner of the Boston Red Sox, did not have so many shows that were financial failures many aspects of Baseball history might have been different. The financially-troubled Frazee was forced to sell Babe Ruth and a number of other Red Sox stars in order to continue the operation of the Red Sox and his Broadway productions. New York Yankee owner Jacob Ruppert paid $100,000 for Ruth on January 3, 1920. In addition, Frazee also obtained a personal loan for $350,000 from Ruppert with Fenway Park as the collateral. Ruppert also paid Frazee $500,000 for Red Sox players Waite Hoyt, Carl Mays, Joe Dugan, Wally Schang, Joe Bush, and Herb Pennock. All of these players became integral parts of

Publisher: Mason Bros. & Co., Boston, MA, Card No. 3077 * Manufacturer: Not Indicated * Type: Pre-Linen * Postmark: Boston, MA, January 22, 1916 * Value Index: B

the Yankee championship teams. Ironically, a few years after Frazee sold his star players to the Yankees he became rich with a Broadway production of "No, No, Nanette." Frazee admitted that he made more than $3,000,000 and would not have sold his players if the money had come earlier. This photograph shows the Red Sox players warming up in front of the grandstand behind home plate prior to a World Series game. If Frazee had been able to retain his best players, many of the Pennants won by the Yankees might have been at Fenway Park.

Heinie Zimmerman had a fine 13-year career with the Chicago Cubs and the New York Giants. His best year was the amazing 1912 season as a Cub infielder. He played every position except pitcher and catcher, but mainly second and third base. Zimmerman led the National League with 207 BHs, a .372 BA, and 14 HRs. His 99 RBI were only 3 behind league leader Honus Wagner. When he was traded to the New York Giants in 1916, Zimmerman led the league in RBI. His performance in 1917 helped the Giants win the National League Championship, although they lost the World Series four games to two against the Chicago White Sox.

HEINE ZIMMERMAN, CHICAGO (Cubs)

Publisher: United States Publishing House, Chicago, IL * Manufacturer: Not Indicated *
Type: Sepia & White * Postmark: Not Used * Value Index: B

RICHARD (RUBE) MARQUARD, NEW YORK (Giants)

When lefthanded pitcher Rube Marquard joined the New York Giants in 1908 he was named "The $11,000 Beauty." The title was based on the fact that he had been purchased from the Indianapolis Club of the American Association for that amount, an unheard-of sum of money for a player. He did not become an instant star with the Giants. In fact, he was defeated in his only 1908 pitching start after his purchase. The New York press began referring to him as "The $11,000 Lemon." In 1909 he won 6 and lost 13 games. Manager John McGraw recognized Marquard's problem and he stated in his book My Thirty Years In Baseball ". . . it was his nervousness over living up to a great reputation that seemed to upset him. As a result he developed problems in controlling his pitches. So fearful was he of not being able to get the ball over when it came down to two and three that he would simply toss it over straight as a string. In other words he had so much stuff that he was afraid to use it." After Marquard mastered control of his pitching, which required two full seasons, he became one of the best pitchers in Baseball. He won 25 and lost 7 games in 1911 and in 1912 he won 27 games. He was almost perfect in the 1912 World Series against the Boston Red Sox allowing only one run in 18 innings and winning 2 games. In 1913 he had 24 wins and 10 losses and he completed his 18-year career in 1925 with 205 victories. "The $11,000 Beauty" was elected to the Hall of Fame in 1971.

Publisher: United States Publishing House, Chicago, IL * Manufacturer: Not Indicated *
Type: Sepia & White * Postmark: Not Used * Value Index: B

This photograph shows the second game of the 1912 World Series between the New York Giants and the Boston Red Sox at Fenway Park. The scene is historically significant because the game ended in a 6 to 6 score. This game was the second time that a tie score had occurred in World Series play. The ball parks did not have lights in 1912 and the Umpires had the right to call a game when it became too dark to continue. Umpire Silk O'Loughlin had to declare the game at an end after 11 innings. Giants ace pitcher Christy Mathewson probably deserved a better fate; however, five costly errors prevented him from from winning a game that would have tied the Series. The extra game enabled the gate receipts to reach almost $500,000, a record

Publisher: Not Indicated * Manufacturer: Not Indicated * Type: Real Photograph * Postmark: Boston, MA, October 12, 1912 * Value Index: A

to that date. The Red Sox players each received a winning share of $4,024 while the losing Giants each received $2,566. Both were record-high payments for a number of years. The game had been played on October 9 and this Postcard was mailed on October 12, showing how quickly Postcards could be produced.

When Charley Ebbets, owner of the Brooklyn Dodgers, was building his new Baseball stadium in 1912 he had financial difficulties and was afraid that he would not be able to complete the project. He asked the McKeever brothers, Steve and Ed, whose contracting company was building the stadium for $100,000. The money was intended for the completion of the park and he gave the McKeever brothers one-half ownership of the team. Ebbets Field was completed and became the home of the Dodgers from April 9, 1913 through September 24, 1957 when they moved to Los Angeles. This photograph shows Ebbets Field when it was completed in 1913. The horses in the foreground remained a reliable form of transportation as

Publisher: APC Co., New York, NY * Manufacturer: Not Indicated * Type: Pre-Linen * Postmark: Brooklyn, NY, May 14, 1915 * Value Index: A

the automobile was not available to most people. Ebbets Field was large: 419 feet along the left field foul line, 450 feet to center field, and 301 feet along the right field foul line.

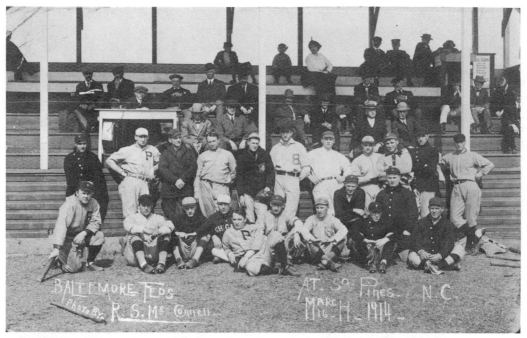

Publisher: R.S. McConnell, Southern Pines, NC * Manufacturer: R.S. McConnell * Type: Real Photograph * Postmark: Not Used * Value Index: A

Publisher: V.O. Hammon Publishing Co., Chicago, IL, Card No. 2261 * Manufacturer: V.O. Hammon * Type: Pre-Linen * Postmark: Not Used * Value Index: B

Originally organized in 1913 as an independent league in the Midwest, the Federal League consisted of six teams: Chicago, Cleveland, Covington (Kentucky), Indianapolis, Pittsburgh, and St. Louis. John T. Powers of Chicago was elected president of the Federal League. The Covington franchise was moved to Kansas City in June 1913. Because the remainder of the League was successful they decided to expand to eight teams for 1914, and they replaced their president with another Chicagoan, James A. Gilmore. He had grandiose plans to compete with the National and American Leagues. At that time the Baseball Reserve Clause which enabled teams to control and reserve players after their contracts had expired was in effect. On August 2, 1913, the Federal League held a secret meeting, deciding to invade the East Coast by adding teams in Baltimore and Brooklyn, to ignore the Reserve Clause, and to sign Major League players not under contract. Player-manager George Stovall of the St. Louis Browns signed for the same position with Kansas City and became the first player to ignore the Reserve Clause. Others followed and many big-name players joined the Federal League. Philadelphia Phillies second baseman Otto Knabe became the Baltimore Terrapins player-manager with a three-year contract at $30,000, three times the sum he was making with the Phillies. This photograph of the Terrapins, providing the earliest known Postcard of a Federal League Team, shows the beginning of Spring Training on March 11, 1914 at Southern Pines, NC. Note the many different Major League uniforms worn by the players as the Terrapin uniforms with their logo had not arrived. Player-Manager Otto Knabe on the left is kneeling holding a bat. One month later the team began their season at the new Terrapin Park.

A team called the Whales, owned by John Weeghman, was the Chicago entry into the Federal League. To build a ball park for his team, Weeghman hired Zachary Taylor Davis, who had designed Comiskey Park, to design a ball park for the land at Clark and Addison Streets on the North Side of Chicago. It was completed for the 1914 season and Weeghman Park was recognized as one of the finest parks in Baseball. This photograph was taken at the grand opening of the Park on April 23, 1914 with a standing-room-only crowd of 15,000 fans. The Federal League was able to attract many star players from the Major Leagues. Chicago Cubs' shortstop Joe Tinker joined the Whales as player-manager and he guided them to 87 wins and 67 losses, 1-1/2 games behind Pennant-winning Indianapolis. In 1915 Tinker won the Pennant by one percentage point over St. Louis: Chicago had 86 wins and 66 losses for a percentage of .566 and St. Louis had 87 wins and 67 losses for .565. The Federal League ended in 1915 because the owners in all three Major Leagues lost money in the salary war and many of the Federal teams merged with the teams in the other Leagues. John Weeghman became the owner of the Chicago Cubs and the team moved into Weeghman Park, abandoning the antiquated West Side Park. Weeghman Park is now known as Wrigley Field.

The Baltimore Terrapins were a charter member of the Federal League. During the mid-1890s, the Orioles were the best team in Baseball. They won National League Pennants in 1894, 1895, and 1896 including star third baseman John McGraw, shortstop Hughie Jennings, catcher and captain Wilbert Robinson, right fielder Wee Willie Keeler, and left fielder Joe Kelley; all of these players entered the Hall of Fame. Ned Hanlon was the innovative manager. Many of these stars were sold to Brooklyn after the 1898 season, and the Dodgers won Pennants in 1899 and 1900. Baltimore was out after the 1899 season having lost its best talent, however, two years later it became a charter member of the American League. After ending the 1902 season in last place they were sold to New York management,

Terrapin Park, Federal League, Baltimore, Md.

Publisher: The Chessler Co., Baltimore, MD, Card No. 2749 * Manufacturer: Not Indicated * Type: Pre-Linen * Postmark: Not Used * Value Index: A

became the Highlanders, and then the Yankees. This photograph was taken on April 13, 1914 and shows Terrapin Park filled with 30,000 fans, the largest crowd in Baltimore Baseball history. Terrapin Park cost $90,000 to construct and was made of wood.

In addition to Brooklyn, the Federal League's status as a third Major League was greatly enhanced by another team in the New York area. The Indianapolis Champions of 1914 were moved to Newark, NJ before the 1915 season. The team's new owner was oil millionaire Harry Sinclair. A new park was built in the suburb of Harrison, named Harrison Park or Peppers Park, and designed by C.B. Comstock, at a cost of slightly more than $100,000. The left and right field foul lines were 375 feet and the distance to the center field bleachers was 450 feet. The ball park had a bicycle track which circled the playing field. Bicycle races were held in conjunction with the Baseball games to

A GAME AT THE NEWARK FEDERAL LEAGUE GROUNDS, NEWARK, N. J.

Publisher: M. Seidl, Newark, NJ * Manufacturer: Superior * Type: Pre-Linen * Postmark: Not Used * Value Index: A

increase attendance. Newark fans were hoping the team would duplicate its 1914 Pennant; however, they finished in fourth place.

When it opened on August 18, 1915, Braves Field was proudly proclaimed as the largest Baseball park in the world. The capacity was approximately 45,000 persons. The Opening day had 56,000 fans in the field plus 6,000 persons turned away. A World Series was played at Braves Field in 1915. The Braves generously allowed the Red Sox to use their new field, which seated 10,000 more fans than Fenway Park, in return for the prior use of Fenway Park in 1914. The claim for the finest and largest stadium was maintained by the Braves until Yankee Stadium was built in 1923. The Braves remained competitive for a few years finishing in second place in 1915, and third place in 1916. They fell to sixth place in 1917, seventh place in 1918, and

BRAVES FIELD, BOSTON LARGEST BASEBALL PARK IN THE WORLD Approximate Cost $1,000,000; Seating Capacity 45,000
BOSTON NATIONAL LEAGUE

COPYRIGHT, 1915, RILEY PHOTOGRAPH CO.   PUBLISHED BY RUGE & BADGER, 194 BOYLSTON ST., BOSTON

Publisher: Ruge & Badger, Boston, MA * Manufacturer: Not Indicated * Type: Pre-Linen * Postmark: Not Used * Value Index: A

last place in 1922 and 1924. The Braves did not win a Pennant until 1948. In the interim, the Red Sox were winning Pennants in 1915, 1916, and 1918 capturing the hearts of Boston fans. Many people thought that Braves Field never had the homey environment of Fenway Park.

This photograph of the first base and right field area of Braves Field provides a good perspective of the Park's large dimensions. The left field and right field walls were 402 feet from home plate and the center field wall was 550 feet away from home plate. Braves Field was built at a cost of $600,000 with the money raised by Arthur C. Wise, a Boston Broker who had completed the financing of Fenway Park three years earlier. Brave Field required 8,200,000 pounds of concrete to build a covered grandstand to seat 18,000 fans, two uncovered pavilions each to seat 10,000 fans, and the famous "Jury Box," in right field, holding 2,000 persons. Braves Field did not hold the interest of the

BRAVES FIELD, LARGEST BALL GROUNDS IN THE WORLD, BOSTON, MASS.

Publisher: Mason Bros. & Co., Boston, MA * Manufacturer: Curt Teich, Chicago, IL * Type: Pre-Linen * Postmark: Boston, MA, May 18, 1917 * Value Index: B

Boston Baseball Fans as Fenway Park did because the seats were far away from the action. As long-time Baseball writer Harold Kaese said, "No matter what alterations various owners made to Braves Field they could never figure out a way to move 8,200,000 pounds of concrete stands closer to the playing field."

This photograph of the new Braves Field is on the only known Postcard showing the exterior view of the field. The building in the foreground was used as offices for the team. The park was built on land that had been the Allston Golf Course on Commonwealth Avenue only a few blocks north of Fenway Park. This site gave the fans excellent access to the Boston Trolley lines which ran in front of the park. The building with the stucco roof shown in the photograph was located on Gaffney Street and it contained ticket arcades. The fans would pass through the arcades on their way to the seats in the right field pavilion or the main grandstand. This building is now used by the Boston University Athletic Department and is the only portion of Braves Field that remains today.

Entrance to Braves Field, Boston, Mass.

Publisher: A. Isreakson & Company, Roxbury, MA * Manufacturer: Not Indicated * Type: Pre-Linen * Postmark: Boston, MA, May 18, 1917 * Value Index: C

Published by The Sporting News   Walter Johnson-Charles Street, Washington, A.L.

This Postcard of Walter Johnson and his catcher Gabby Street was issued by the Sporting News in 1915. The hard-throwing righthander was considered the fastest and best pitcher in Baseball. He had the highest number of wins in the American League for four consecutive seasons with 34 games in 1913, and 28 games in 1914 and 1915, and 25 games in 1916. When Johnson ended his pitching career in 1927 he had also led the League with 23 wins in 1923 and 1924. Gabby Street had left the Washington Senators in 1911 before this Postcard was issued. The photograph must have been taken during that last season with Washington. Street caught 28 games with the New York Highlanders in 1912. He retired as an active player in 1931 when he made one appearance as a catcher with the St. Louis Cardinals, where he was a manager. He was considered a brilliant handler of pitchers and helped to develop Johnson. He achieved fame as the first man to catch a baseball thrown out of the Washington Monument 550 feet above the ground. This feat had been tried by other players including William Schriver, a Catcher with the Chicago Colts, in 1894. Twelve balls were thrown out to Street and all hit a wall of the monument on the way down. He caught the 13th ball over his head, then staggered as the impact almost drove his glove into the ground, yet held onto the ball to achieve his fame.

Publisher: The Sporting News, St. Louis, MO * Manufacturer: Not Indicated * Type: Pre-Linen * Postmark: Not Used * Value Index: A

Baker Bowl was named after the owner of the Philadelphia Phillies, William F. Baker, and was the home of the Phillies from May 2, 1895 to June 30, 1938, when the team moved into Shibe Park. This photograph captures a bygone era when fans were informed by a park announcer using a megaphone. The Baker Bowl shown in this illustration was reconstructed in 1895 after a fire destroyed a major portion of the grandstand. The site was on Huntingdon and Broad Streets, only a few blocks from the location where Shibe Park was placed. The left field seats are 335 feet and the right field fence is only 275 feet from home plate. Left-handed batters had a definite advantage at the Baker Bowl. In 1915 the Phillies played in their only World Series at the Baker Bowl. The lone bright spot for the Phillies was the outstanding pitching of Grover Cleveland Alexander, who allowed only five hits in winning the World Series opener by a 3 to 1 score. They lost the Series to the Boston Red Sox four games to one.

PHILADELPHIA BALL PARK OF NATIONAL LEAGUE, PHILADELPHIA, PA.

Publisher: Not Indicated, Card No. 222179 * Manufacturer: Not Indicated * Type: Pre-Linen * Postmark: Not Used * Value Index: B

Some Major League Baseball players became more famous after their playing careers were over. Reverend Billy Sunday was an example. He spent his eight-year career, from 1893 to 1890, as a reserve outfielder with the Chicago White Stockings, Pittsburgh Pirates, and Philadelphia Phillies and had only a lifetime .248 BA. As a fire-and-brimstone evangelist he became famous all over the world. Dr. William T. Ellis, who wrote Sunday's authorized biography in 1917 said, "Some of the platform activities of Sunday made spectators gasp. He raced to and fro across the platform. No posture was too extreme for this restless gymnast."

As a ball player, Sunday had great speed and was considered one of the finest defensive outfielders of the day. As an example, in 1886 the White Stockings met the Detroit Wolverines in a game that would decide the Pennant. With two runners on base and two out in the ninth inning, Chicago was leading by one run. Detroit's Charley Bennett hit a long fly ball to the outfield that appeared to be a definite base hit. Sunday raced after the ball and made an outstanding catch to save the game for Chicago. Ecstatic fans took up a collection and presented Sunday with $1,500 to show their appreciation.

Publisher: Irving Klein, New York, NY * Manufacturer: Not Indicated * Type: Black & White * Postmark: Not Used * Value Index: B

Copyrighted 1917, by International Film Co.

BILLY SUNDAY The Baseball Evangelist Preacher

REDLAND FIELD, CINCINNATI, O.

Publisher: O.A. Boeckley, Latonia, KY * Manufacturer: Not Indicated * Type: Black & White * Postmark: Not Used * Value Index: A

The infamous "Black Sox Scandal" rocked Baseball to its foundation when it became known that eight members of the Chicago White Sox had taken money from gamblers to lose the 1919 World Series to the Cincinnati Reds. The eight tainted players were superstar outfielder Shoeless Joe Jackson, pitchers Eddie Cicotte and Claude "Lefty" Williams, first baseman Chick Gandil, shortstop Swede Risberg, third baseman Buck Weaver, outfielder Happy Felsch, and utilityman Fred McMullin. Despite winning an American League Pennant and World Series Championship in 1917 with basically the same team, the owner, Charles Comiskey, was not generous with his players' salaries and the players constantly grumbled about their poor pay. When gamblers approached the players and suggested conspiring to fix games they all agreed. Jackson asked for $20,000 but received only $5,000, Gandil, the ringleader, received $20,000, and Cicotte found $10,000 under his pillow before the first game at Redland Field. Although these payments seemed enormous at that time the gamblers reportedly made more than $500,000. All the details of the case were not presented in the 1920 trial of the eight players and they were acquitted. Baseball Commissioner Kenesaw Mountain Landis banned them from the game for life. This photograph of the first game at Redland Field shows an overflow crowd watching the underdog Reds wallop 29-game winner Cicotte by a 9 to 1 score. Cicotte's performance of lobbing pitches to batters aroused suspicion that something was amiss. When Cincinnati won five games to three, the 1919 White Sox were tainted forever as the "Black Sox."

In 1919 Eddie Roush led the world champion Cincinnati Reds and the National League with his .321 BA. He was a superb defensive outfielder during his 18-year career. He had a lifetime .323 BA and earned a place in the Hall of Fame. Although the Reds' World Series victory over the Chicago White Sox may be tainted because of the Black Sox scandal the Reds had a fine team that won 96 games to finish six games ahead of the second place New York Giants. Many people say that if the World Series had been played honestly the Reds would have won the World Series on their own merits.

Publisher: Not Indicated * Manufacturer: Not Indicated * Type: Black & White * Postmark: Not Used * Value Index: B

EDDIE ROUSH, *Center Field*
Cincinnati "Reds" World's Champions 1919

HARRY SALLEE, *Pitcher*
Cincinnati "Reds" World's Champions 1919

Pitcher Harry "Slim" Sallee, a 6-foot-3-inch lefthander enjoyed his finest Major League season in 1919 by playing a key role in the Cincinnati Reds winning the National League Pennant. Sallee won 21 and lost 7 games in the regular season and won 1 and lost 1 game in the World Series against the Chicago White Sox. The Reds won the Series five games to three. In the Series game that he lost, his teammates made four errors as Chicago won by a 4 to 1 score, he won the second game by a 4 to 2 score in 13-1/3 innings.

Sallee had a 1.35 ERA in postseason play. His Major League career ended in 1921 with the New York Giants when he won 6 and lost 4 games as a relief pitcher. His sidearm delivery baffled National League hitters for 14 seasons as he compiled a record of 172 wins and 143 losses.

Publisher: Not Indicated * Manufacturer: Not Indicated * Type: Black & White * Postmark: Not Used * Value Index: C

92   American League, "White Sox" Ball Park, Chicago.

Publisher: Gerson Bros., Chicago, IL, Card No. 92, 1960 * Manufacturer: Not Indicated * Type: Pre-Linen * Postmark: Chicago, IL, December 27, 1914 * Value Index: C

Photographs used on Postcards are frequently altered by the Postcard publisher to enhance the appearance of the Postcard, increase sales, and for public relations purposes. The two Postcards of Comiskey Park shown here have one important difference. The lower Postcard shows the addition of Charles A. Comiskey, owner of the Chicago White Sox, leaning against the rail. From a speculation standpoint Comiskey may have been added to the second Postcard because he was angry that he had not been included in the first Postcard. Perhaps, the publisher may have decided to add him to the second Postcard to gain favor from Comiskey for future work that was planned.

581. American League, " Sox " Ball Park, Chicago.

Publisher: Not Indicated, Card No. 581 * Manufacturer: Not Indicated * Type: Pre-Linen * Postmark: Not Used * Value Index: C

This interior view of League Park in Cleveland shows the Park during the 1920 World Series between the Cleveland Indians and the Brooklyn Dodgers. The death of shortstop Ray Champman dampened the excitment of the Pennant-winning season. The Indians were in first place on August 16 and were at the Polo Grounds to face the New York Yankees who were 1-1/2 games behind in second place. Pitcher Carl Mays was a submarining righthander and Chapman was a right-hand batter who crowded the home plate. Chapman was leading off the top of the fifth inning when Mays threw his underarm delivery high and inside. Chapman seemed to freeze and the ball hit him in the temple. He was

League Baseball Park, Cleveland, Ohio.

Publisher: J. Sapirstein, Cleveland, OH, Card No. 6950 * Manufacturer: Not Indicated * Type: Pre-Linen * Postmark: Cleveland, OH, February 13, 1921 * Value Index: B

rushed to a hospital where he died the next morning. When the season was over, the Indians dedicated themselves to winning the World Series for Ray Chapman. They beat the Brooklyn Dodgers 5 games to 2.

This illustration shows how Baseball fans followed the fortunes of their favorite teams before the advent of radio and television. Large electric scoreboards were set up in downtown locations for huge crowds to watch. In Brooklyn, during the 1920 World Series with Cleveland, a scoreboard was placed on the corner of Fulton Street and Dekalb Avenue. After this Postcard was published, the proprietor of the store imprinted the Postcard to promote clothing sales for men. For example, a $50.00 suit could be purchased for $42.50, a $40.00 suit was available for $33.50, etc. Most of the Brooklyn fans were disappointed with the results of the World Series; hopefully, the proprietor of the store had better results with his sale.

Where Brooklyn Watched the World's Series, Fulton St. at DeKalb Ave., Brooklyn, N. Y.

Publisher: E.C. Kropp Co., Milwaukee, WI, Card No. 29519N * Manufacturer: E.C. Kropp Co. * Type: Pre-Linen * Postmark: Brooklyn, NY, July 20, 1922 * Value Index: B

This photograph of Ebbets Field, taken in 1920, shows the front entrance to the park. This view continued to be the most popular with the primary change being the people standing in front of it. park. When Ebbets Field opened in 1913 the Brooklyn fans did not have a long wait for a Pennant. In 1916, under the direction of Wilbert Robinson, the Dodgers won their first Pennant at the new park. First baseman Jake Daubert led with a .316 BA and Zach Wheat had a .312 BA. Jeff Pfeffer led the Dodger pitchers with 25 wins. The Dodgers lost the World Series to the Boston Red Sox four games to one. One of the Boston victories was recorded by lefthander Babe Ruth who was to achieve greater fame a few years later as a slug-

EBBETS FIELD.   BROOKLYN, NEW YORK.

Publisher: The Long Island News Co., Long Island, NY * Manufacturer: The Albertype Co., Brooklyn, NY * Type: Black & White * Postmark: Not Used * Value Index: A

ging outfielder for the New York Yankees. In 1920, spitball pitcher Burleigh Grimes had 23 wins and led the Dodgers to another Pennant, but they lost to Cleveland in the World Series.

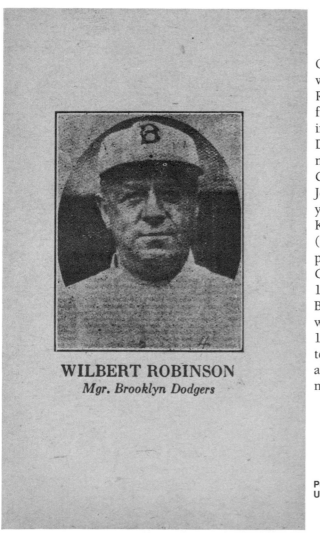

WILBERT ROBINSON
Mgr. Brooklyn Dodgers

Wilbert Robinson and John McGraw played for the famous Baltimore Orioles who dominated Baseball throughout most of the 1890s. Robinson was the veteran catcher and McGraw the third baseman. Although Robinson was 10 years older than McGraw they became the best of friends and partners in a combination gym, restaurant, and bowling alley in Baltimore, called The Diamond. Duckpin bowling originated at The Diamond. To save money when the larger pins became damaged the partners shaved them down to a smaller size and continued to use them. Customers preferred them and the idea spread to other parts of the U.S. John McGraw became manager of the New York Giants in 1902 and one year later Robinson joined him as his principal coach amd confidant. Known as " Uncle Robbie," Robinson was as kind-hearted as he was large (his weight grew to almost 300 pounds from his playing weight of 215 pounds). Robinson spent most of his time developing pitchers including Christy Mathewson, Rube Marquard, and Joe McGinnity. At the end of 1913 Robinson resigned as the Giants Coach and became manager of the Brooklyn Dodgers. The friendship had passed to the point where they were not speaking to each other. His career as Dodger manager lasted for 19 years and ended in 1931 with 1,397 wins and 1,395 losses. This photograph was taken in 1924. He died on August 8, 1934, only six months after McGraw. They are buried only a few yards apart, achieving a closeness that had eluded them in their later years.

Publisher: Not Indicated * Manufacturer: Not Indicated * Type: Black & White * Postmark: Not Used * Value Index: A

Every Baseball broadcaster during these past 70 years owes a debt of graditude to Harold W. Arlin shown in the upper-left corner of this illustration. He was the concert announcer for radio station KDKA in Pittsburgh when he became the first announcer for a Baseball game on August 5, 1921. Arlin spoke into a telephone that had been converted into a microphone by Westinghouse Engineers to describe the game between the Pittsburgh Pirates and Philadelphia Phillies at Forbes Field in Pittsburgh. An important aspect of this broadcast was that it was accomplished from a box seat located at ground level. The elevated radio and TV booths of today did not exist. At the time of his broadcast, Arlin was working as a foreman for Westinghouse and moonlighting for the company-owned station in the evening. Arlin was also the first person to broadcast the Davis Cup tennis matches and a football game between Pittsburgh and West Virginia played that Fall at Pittsburgh Stadium. His work in sports and other duties was so good that KDKA gave him the title "First Full-Time Radio Announcer In The World." In later years, reflecting on the initial broadcast years, Arlin modestly said,"No one had the foggiest idea, the slightest hint of an inkling, that what we started would take off like it did."

Publisher: Westinghose Electric Co., Pittsburgh, PA, Card No. O.C.1543 * Manufacturer: Not Indicated * Type: Sepia & White * Postmark: Not Used * Value Index: A

Within a short time of the Harold W. Arlin broadcast, Baseball broadcasts were beginning all over the U.S. During the 1921 World Series between the New York Giants and Yankees, radio station WJZ in Newark, New Jersey and WBZ in Springfield, Massachusetts joined to re-create the games on radio. The *Newark Call* reporter Sandy Hunt telephoned the plays from the press box at the Polo Grounds in New York to Thomas Cowan, WJZ program supervisor who described Hunt's comments over the two-station network. During the 1922 Giants and Yankees World Series live play-by-play broadcasts were given by sports writer Grantland Rice of the *New York Tribune* and the color commentary by Graham McNamee. Rice was flustered by the assignment, lasted four innings of the third game, and gave up the microphone to McNamee, who became one of the most famous early network announcers. Years later, Rice told Red Barber of his World Series assignment, "Once was enough for me for all my life." In 1922 there were 3 million radio receivers in the U.S., many of them built by Radio Corporation of America (RCA). This advertising Postcard promotes the RCA Radiola 46 by asking fans to "Tune in and Thrill to the Big Games." The background is an artist's sketch of the Polo Grounds. At the bottom of the Postcard is a space to print information as to where the Radiola 46 was available. These Postcards were used by stores all over the U.S.

Publisher: Radio Corporation of America * Manufacturer: Not Indicated * Type: U.S. Government Postal Card * Postmark: Not Used * Value Index: B

Ken Williams is one of many unfortunate Major League Baseball players who performed most of their careers with a second division ball club and never received their deserved recognition. This photograph was taken in 1922 when Williams had one of the finest seasons in Baseball history with the St. Louis Browns. He hit 39 HRs, a spectacular number at that date, and had a .332 BA with 155 RBI. The Browns finished only one game behind the champion Yankees in that year because of Williams' phenomenal season. Unfortunately, that was the best position reached by any of the Williams' teams. They were last place twice, seventh place four times, fifth place three times, fourth place once, and third place twice. Ken Williams finished his career with the Boston Red Sox in 1929 with a career .319 BA. If he had played on better teams he might have become a member of the Hall of Fame.

Publisher: Exhibit Supply Co., Chicago, IL * Manufacturer: Not Indicated * Type: Sepia & White * Postmark: Not Used * Value Index: B

When New York Giants manager John McGraw wrote his autobiography in 1923 he selected Ray Schalk as the finest catcher in the American League. He said, "Schalk is a hard and accurate thrower and because of a wonderful pair of hands he is seldom disabled. He is also very fast on the bases and is a good hitter. I regard him as the best backstop the American League has ever produced." Born in Harvel, Illinois on August 12, 1892, Schalk was signed by the Chicago White Sox in 1912. He was considered too small for Baseball by many people. He proved them wrong as he caught over 100 games per season during eleven consecutive seasons leading all catchers in putouts and assists. An excellent handler of pitchers he caught four no hitters during his 18-year career and had a lifetime .253 BA. An innovator, Schalk was the first catcher to back up plays at first base and third base and on several occasions made putouts at second base. When his career ended with the White Sox, McGraw signed him to a Giants contract for 1929. Schalk was elected to the Hall of Fame in 1955.

Publisher: Exhibit Supply Co., Chicago, IL * Manufacturer: Not Indicated * Type: Sepia & White * Postmark: Not Used * Value Index: B

Jack Bentley has been called "the Babe Ruth of the International League" and in many respects it is an apt description. Ruth and Bentley were natives of Maryland and they were excellent pitchers and batters. Bentley joined the Washington Senators in 1913 as an 18-year old high school wonder from Sandy Springs, Maryland. During his rookie year Bentley was in three games pitching 11 innings, allowing 5 hits and no runs, and had one win and no games lost. In 1914 he had a 2.37 ERA as a starting and relief pitcher with 5 wins and 8 losses. Unfortunately, many Senator pitchers did not have the necessary hitting support from their teammates. In 1915 Bentley had a brilliant 0.79 ERA and no wins and 2 losses for the 4 games that he pitched. In 1916 he was sent to the Baltimore Orioles of the International League where he had lasting fame. As a pitcher-first baseman he was a key member of the team that won seven consecutive International League Pennants. In 1921 he was the only player in the League's history to lead in batting and pitching with a .412 BA and 12 wins and only one loss. In 1922 the New York Giants paid Orioles owner Jack Dunn the record sum of $72,500 to purchase Bentley's contract. In 1923 Bentley won 13 and lost 8 games to help the Giants win the Pennant and in 1924 he won 16 and lost 5 games. As this illustration indicates during his off seasons Bentley sold Cole Aero Eight automobiles.

JACK BENTLEY
NOW SELLING THE
COLE AERO - EIGHT
THE NEELY - ENSOR - FOX AUTO CO.
MT. ROYAL AVE. cor. McMECHEN ST.

Publisher: I & M Ottenheimer, Baltimore, MD * Manufacturer: Not Indicated * Type: Black & White * Postmark: Not Used * Value Index: A

A Baseball Game at the Polo Grounds as seen from an airship. New York

This marvelous photograph of the Polo Grounds was taken from an airship and it shows the park in the 1920s when it had a seating capacity of approximately 45,000 persons. The centerfield area was spacious with the left and right field seats close to home plate. It was 279 feet along the left field foul line, 257 feet along the right field foul line, and 483 feet out to centerfield.

The second deck in left field hung over the lower deck by 23 feet. A high fly ball along the foul lines to either right or left field, over 250 feet, was usually a HR. One of the frustrating feelings for an outfielder was to go back to the wall and watch helplessly as a ball he could have caught dropped into the second deck because of the overhang.

Publisher: Manhatten Postcard Co., New York, NY, Card No. 9997 * Manufacturer: Not Indicated * Type: Pre-Linen * Postmark: Not Used * Value Index: C

Yankee Stadium has been called "The House That Ruth Built." George Herman "Babe" Ruth of the New York Yankees was larger than life and the dominant star of Baseball for nearly two decades. More than 40 years after his death in 1948, he remains the best known personality in Baseball history. His popularity and HR exploits made him Baseball's greatest attraction in the 1920s when the Yankees shared the Polo Grounds with the New York Giants. It was infuriating to Giants' manager John McGraw that the Yankees had more fans, because of Ruth, despite the fact that both teams were winning Pennants and the Giants beat the Yankees in the 1921 and 1922 World Series. McGraw wanted Ruth and the Yankees out of the Polo Grounds

THE YANKEE STADIUM, NEW YORK CITY.

Publisher: Manhattan Postcard Co., New York, NY, Card No. 42,116096 * Manufacturer: Tichnor Bros., Cambridge, MA * Type: Pre-Linen * Postmark: New York, NY, September 6, 1924 * Value Index: C

and Jake Ruppert, Yankee owner, responded by building the largest and finest baseball facility directly across the Harlem River from the Polo Grounds. This artist's drawing of a proposed design was reproduced on the earliest-known Postcard of Yankee Stadium. It shows a fully enclosed structure. During the construction the design was changed to include open center-field bleachers. Yankee Stadium opened on April 18, 1923 with the right field fence only 295 feet from home plate designed exactly for Ruth's HR swing. He hit 41 HRs during 1923 and was building to his record of 60 HRs in 1927. When Ruth set the HR record in 1927, 32 of his HRs occurred while the team was on the road showing that he could hit HRs in any stadium.

This illustration shows Yankee Stadium on opening day, April 18, 1923, and the original design of the stadium completely enclosed. The designer was the Osborn Engineering Company, Cleveland, OH, and the builder was the White Engineering Company, New York, NY. The huge stadium was built in 284 days and covers 10 acres in the Bronx between 157th and 161st Streets and from River Avenue to the Major Deegan Expressway. Officially there were 74,200 fans inside the stadium for the grand opening while 20,000 fans waited outside, clamoring to get in. They went away disappointed when the gates were locked. The people inside were entertained by the music of the Seventh Regiment Band, directed by John Phillip Sousa. For many fans the best music was the sound

YANKEE STADIUM NEW YORK

Publisher: Pictorial News Co., New York, NY, Card No. NY440, * Manufacturer: Not Indicated * Type: Pre-Linen * Postmark: Not Used * Value Index: B

of Babe Ruth's bat hitting a three-run homer as the Yankee beat Boston by a score of 4 to 1. As the *New York Times* reported the next day, "The biggest crowd in baseball history rose to its feet and let loose the biggest shout in baseball history after Ruth's dramatic home run."

When Yankee Stadium opened in 1923 it was to become the most famous Baseball stadium in America. It was the newest stadium, the home of Babe Ruth, and a tourist attraction. In 1923 the Yankees won their first World Series Championship. Ruth hit 41 HRs, had 140 RBI, and a .393 BA which was the highest in Ruth's career. Amazingly, Harry Heilman of Detroit had a .403 BA to capture the 1923 American League batting title. This photograph of the front entrance was taken in 1927. The 1927 Yankees had Ruth leading a cast of sluggers referred to as "Murderers Row." First baseman Lou Gehrig had 47 HRs and led the American League with 140 RBI. Ruth hit 60 HRs, a career record which was not broken until 1961 by another Yankee, Roger Maris. Second baseman

YANKEE STADIUM, NEW YORK.

Publisher: Haberman's, Bronx, NY, Card No. 224,24828 Manufacturer: Haberman's * Type: Pre-Linen * Postmark: Not Used * Value Index: C

Tony Lazzeri hit 18 HRs and had 102 RBI. The pitching staff that was headed by righthander Waite Hoyt who won 22 and lost 7 games. In the 1927 World Series they demolished a fine Pittsburgh team in four games.

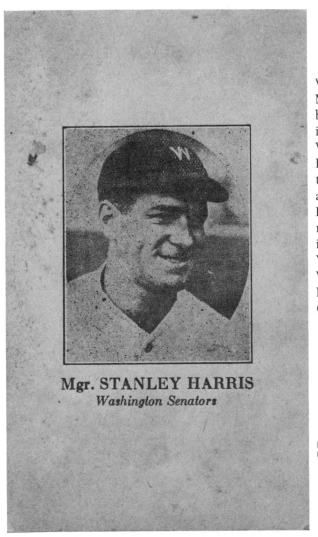

Mgr. STANLEY HARRIS
Washington Senators

In 1924 Stanley "Bucky" Harris became player-manager of the Washington Senators at 27 years of age and was named "The Boy Manager." Washington owner Clark Griffith selected his standout second baseman because of his leadership ability. The move proved to be fortuitous for the Senators won the American League Pennant and became World Champions by defeating the New York Giants four games to three. Harris batted .333 in the World Series, scoring 5 runs with 7 RBI to lead the team. The Senators repeated as American League Champions in 1925 and lost the World Series to the Pittsburgh Pirates four games to three. Bucky's 12-year playing career ended in 1931 with a lifetime .274 BA. His managerial career spanned 29 seasons with six different teams and ended in 1956 with the Detroit Tigers. In 1947, as a manager of the New York Yankees, he won his third Pennant and second World Championship. Washington fans will always be indebted to Harris as the 1924 "Boy Manager" who brought the only World Championship to the Nation's Capitol.

Publisher: Not Indicated * Manufacturer: Not Indicated * Type: Black & White * Postmark: Not Used * Value Index: A

In the early 1920s the New York Giants and Manager John McGraw were the toast of New York, with the names McGraw and Giants being synonymous. This photograph, taken in the 1920s, shows the grandstand viewed from right field with a cameo of McGraw. The team was referred to as "McGraw's Giants." The Giants won the pennant for three consecutive seasons beginning in 1921 and played the Yankees in the World Series during that time. McGraw defeated the Yankees in 1921 and 1922. He was more than a Baseball man, socializing with Broadway producers, actors, and song writers, many of whom were his closest friends. George M. Cohan wrote the Introduction to McGraw's autobiography in

Polo Grounds, National League Baseball Park, New York.

Publisher: UPC Co., Card No. 42 * Manufacturer: Not Indicated * Type: Pre-Linen * Postmark: Not Used * Value Index: C

1923, "It wasn't an easy matter to write an appreciation of John J. McGraw. There's so much in the man to appreciate. So many fine things which might be said, the life story of the Little Napoleon from the cradle to the 1922 World's Championship. We all know that. So why waste ten or twelve thousand words? Let's get down to what we want to find out. What is it that this man has on the ball? That is the question. The answer is EVERYTHING."

When Forbes Field opened in 1909 the Pittsburgh Pirates won the National League Pennant and the World Series. Unfortunately, it was 16 years later before Forbes Field had another Pennant. In 1925 the Pirates were on top, led by hard-hitting outfielders Kiki Cuyler, Max Carey, and Clyde Barnhart all with over .300 BAs. The Pirates won 95 and lost 58 games finishing 8-1/2 games ahead of the defending National League Champion New York Giants. In addition, third baseman Pie Traynor, catcher Earl Smith, and backup first baseman Stuffy McGinnis all hit above a .300 BA. Pirate pitcher Lee Meadows led with 19 wins, Pitchers Ray Kremer and Johnny Morrison and Emil Yde had 17

ENTRANCE TO FORBES FIELD, PITTSBURGH, PA.

Publisher: I. Robbins & Co., Pittsburgh, PA, Card No. A-65513 * Manufacturer: Randson * Type: Pre-Linen * Postmark: Not Used * Value Index: C

wins, and pitcher Vic Aldridge had 15 wins. The entire team had a .307 BA. Manager Bill McKechnie's team completed this outstanding season with an exciting victory over the defending World Champion Washington Senators in the World Series, four games to three.

This photograph shows Sportsman's Park decorated with the bunting for the 1926 World Series with the mighty New York Yankees. The St. Louis Cardinals were the underdogs in the Series. The Cardinals had won a tight National League race by two games over Cincinnati. The St. Louis fans were understandably wild in their enthusiasm as the city celebrated its first Pennant since the St. Louis Browns accomplished the feat in 1888. The Browns were a member of the American Association, a Major League at the time. The Cardinals had fine power hitters and solid pitching against the Yankee powerhouse. First baseman Sunny Jim Bottomley led the National League with 120 RBI and his 19 HRs was second

Publisher: Not Indicated * Manufacturer: Not Indicated * Type: Real Photograph * Postmark: Not Used * Value Index: D

to the League leading Hack Wilson of the Cubs who had 21 HRs. Third baseman Les Bell led his team with a .325 BA and drove in 100 runs. The pitching of righthander Flint Rhem was the League's best with 20 wins. The hero of the 1926 World Series was 37-year-old veteran pitcher Grover Cleveland Alexander. He won two complete games and relieved in the 7th inning of the deciding game, pitching 2-1/3 shutout innings. This effort gave the Cardinals a long awaited World Series Championship, four games to three.

Babe Ruth was so popular that his nickname brought instant recognition. The message on the reverse side of this Postcard was written by a fan to a friend in "Wooster", Massachusetts, " Hi Jim: Jerry and I saw Babe hit a homer in this park today. X marks the spot where we sat. Harry." The May 23, 1927 postmark indicates that Harry saw Ruth hit the 11th HR of the 1927 season off Washington righthander Sloppy Thurston, as Babe worked toward his record-breaking 60 HRs. This photograph shows Yankee Stadium as it looked in 1927 before the grandstands were double-decked along the left field foul line in 1928. The grandstands along the right field foul line were double-decked in 1937.

Publisher: Underwood & Underwood, New York, NY, Card No. 20749 * Manufacturer: Haberman's, Brooklyn, NY * Type: Pre-Linen * Postmark: New York, NY, May 23, 1927 * Value Index: B

In 1928 the St. Louis Cardinals had most of the World Champion players of 1926. They had finished in second place in 1927, 1-1/2 games behind the Pittsburgh Pirates. In 1928, under the guidance of Manager Bill McKechnie the Cardinals won the Pennant two games ahead of the New York Giants. Sunny Jim Bottomley, on the extreme left in the bottom row, had a .325 BA, scored 123 runs, and had 136 RBI. He won the National League Most Valuable Player Award. Left fielder Chick Hafey led the Cardinal regulars with a .336 BA and 111 RBI and Walley Roettger, who later became coach at the University of Illinois, contributed as a reserve outfielder with a .341 BA and 44 RBI in only 68 games. If the Cardinals were looking for a repeat of the 1926

Publisher: Block Bros., St. Louis, MO * Manufacturer: Block Bros. * Type: Real Photograph: * Postmark: Not Used * Value Index: C

triumph over the Yankees they had a disappointment. New York overwhelmed the Cardinals in four straight games as Babe Ruth and Lou Gehrig bombarded St. Louis pitching. Ruth and Gehrig had 13 RBI, more runs than the Cardinals scored during all four games. St. Louis owner Sam Breadon was so upset over the poor showing, he demoted Bill McKechnie to the Cardinals top farm club at Rochester, NY and brought Red Wings player-manager Billy Southworth to replace him for the 1929 season.

Weeghman Park (Wrigley Field) in Chicago was built for the Chicago Whales of the Federal League in 1914. When the Federal League ended in 1915 the park became the property of the National League Cubs and they made extensive renovations. The first changes occurred in 1923 after chewing gum magnate William Wrigley purchased the team and increased the seating from 15,000 to 20,000. During the Winter of 1926-27 the grandstands were double-decked, increasing the seating to 45,000. This photograph was taken after the work of 1926-27. With the Wrigley family ownership and the money available to improve the team the Cubs became Pennant contenders. In 1929 they won their first Pennant since 1910 and had

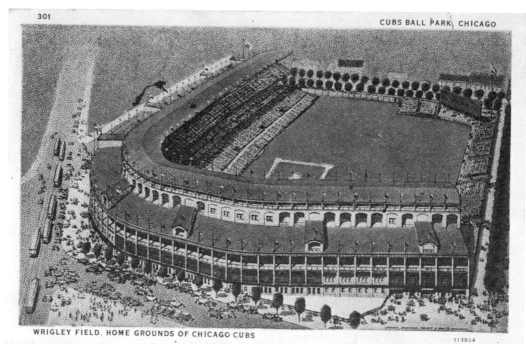

WRIGLEY FIELD, HOME GROUNDS OF CHICAGO CUBS

Publisher: Max Rigot Selling Co., Chicago, IL, Card No. 301,113804 * Manufacturer: Curt Teich, Chicago, IL * Type: Pre-Linen * Postmark: Chicago, IL, June 20, 1929 * Value Index: B

1,485,166 fans, a remarkable attendance for the 1920s. Second baseman Roger Hornsby led the Cub hitters with a .380 BA. Left fielder Riggs Stephenson had a .362 BA and right fielder KiKi Cuyler had a .360 BA. The entire Cub team ended the season with a .303 BA, an outstanding average in any era. Despite this strong team the Cubs lost the 1929 World Series to the Philadelphia Athletics four games to one.

This illustration shows Shibe Park prior to the 1929 season. New seating including 2,500 mezzanine seats was added and one year later the roof was raised for an additional 3,000 seats for an approximate total of 33,000 seats. The Philadelphia Athletics won three consecutive American League Pennants beginning in 1929 and were considered one of the best teams ever assembled. Owner-manager Connie Mack had created oustanding hitting, superb pitching, and excellent defense. The 1927 Yankees were considered the greatest team of all time. In 1928 they were also League Champions and they were expected to repeat in 1929. The Athletics won the Pennant by overpowering the "Bronx Bombers" with an unbelievable 18-game lead. Left fielder Al Simmons led the batting attack with a .365 BA and 157 RBIs. Jimmy Foxx had a .354 BA and 118 RBI, right fielder Bing Miller had a .335 BA, and the versatile Jimmy Dykes batted .337 in a utility role.

152:—Exterior Shibe Baseball Stadium, Philadelphia, Pa.

Publisher: P. Sander, Philadelphia, PA and Atlantic City, NJ * Manufacturer: P. Sander * Type: Pre-Linen * Postmark: Philadelphia, PA, June 15, 1929 * Value Index: A

When the Cleveland Municipal Stadium was completed on July 1, 1931 it was the last and largest stadium built for more than two decades. It held more than 70,000 fans and cost $2,844,000. The Indians waited for more than a year to play ball in their stadium. The first sporting event held there was a boxing match between heavyweight champion Max Schmeling and Young Stribling. On July 31, 1932 the Indians played their first game in the stadium against the defending American League Champion Philadelphia Athletics. In 1933 the Tribe played all of their home games there; however, from 1934 through 1947 only weekend and holiday games were played there. This artist's sketch of Municipal Stadium was available on the Postcard racks two years before the stadium was completed in 1931.

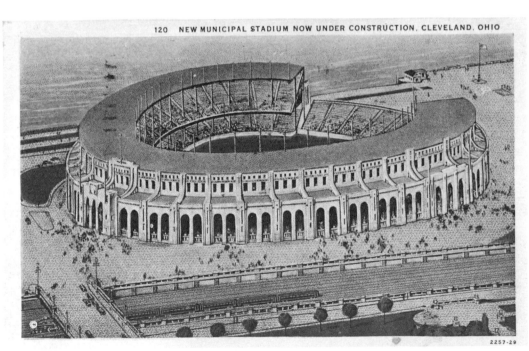

120 NEW MUNICIPAL STADIUM NOW UNDER CONSTRUCTION, CLEVELAND, OHIO

2257-29

Publisher: The Braun Art Publishing Co., Cleveland, OH, Card No. 120,2257-29 * Manufacturer: Curt Teich Co., Chicago, IL * Type: Pre-Linen * Postmark: Cleveland, OH, July 26, 1929 * Value Index: B

This photograph shows the partially completed Cleveland Municipal Stadium on the shore of Lake Erie in 1931. The huge structure required only 370 days to build and was financed by the sale of municipal bonds approved by the voters in 1928. It was the first stadium not built by a team. The Indians did not plan to use it on a regular basis, as they owned League Park where they had been playing since 1910. The seating capacity for 25,000 fans was sufficient to accommodate the regular Cleveland crowds.

Publisher: Brunner State Studios, Inc., Cleveland. OH * Manufacturer: Brunner State Studios, Inc. * Type: Real Photograph * Postmark: Not Used * Value Index: A

On July 31, 1932 a record crowd of 76,979 persons saw the first Major League Baseball game played in the Cleveland Municipal Stadium. The Philadelphia Athletics were the opposition. Manager Connie Mack sent his ace lefthander Lefty Grove to pitch against the Indians. Grove had won 31 games in 1931 and won 25 games in 1932, only one game less than the American League leader General Crowder of Washington. Manager Roger Peckinpaugh selected righthander Mel Harder to pitch for Cleveland. Harder won 13 games in 1931 and 15 games in 1932. The game was a pitching duel and Philadelphia won by a 1 to 0 score. The new stadium was a pitcher's park because of the huge dimensions. The measurements were 322 feet along each

Publisher: Saperstein Greeting Card Co., Cleveland, OH * Manufacturer: Saperstein Greeting Card Co. * Type: Pre-Linen * Postmark: Cleveland, OH, August 21, 1933 * Value Index: B

foul line, then the field spread to 435 feet out on the power alleys, and 470 feet to centerfield. The batters, accustomed to the smaller size of League Park, did not want to play at the new stadium. Years later, the Indians installed fences that cut down the size of the outfield and the stadium became important to long-ball hitters. When Bill Veeck bought control of the Indians in 1947 the playing field was 320 feet along each foul line, 365 feet out on the power alleys, and 410 feet to centerfield.

This photograph shows Yankee Stadium as it looked during the 1932 World Series with the Chicago Cubs. The Postcard had been mailed by a Cub fan a few hours (6:30 PM) after the second game of the overall Series. The Yankees won the game by a 5 to 2 score and the series in four games. Lefty Gomez pitched all nine innings for the Yankees and defeated Lon Warneke who pitched for Chicago. This series was the last for Babe Ruth who hit 2 HRs, had 6 RBI, and scored 6 runs, while Lou Gehrig hit 3 HRs, had 6 RBI, and scored 9 runs.

Yankee Stadium, Bronx, New York.

Publisher: Underwood & Underwood, New York, NY, Card No. 17040 * Manufacturer: Not Indicated * Type: Pre-Linen * Postmark: Morris Heights, NY, September 29, 1932 * Value Index: C

Many Baseball fans do not realize the close proximity of the Polo Grounds, home of the New York Giants and Yankee Stadium, home of the Yankees. This aerial photograph, taken during the 1930s, shows the two locations separated by the Harlem River. The Polo Grounds, located on the left side of the photograph was the site of the National League Giants from 1891 to 1958 when they moved to San Francisco. Yankee Stadium, on the right side of the photograph, opened on April 18, 1923. The fans of the Giants and Yankees did not have far to travel when the two teams played each other in 1923, 1936, and 1937 in the World Series.

Publisher: Not Indicated * Manufacturer: Gravotone Co., New York, NY * Type: Black & White * Postmark * Not Used * Value Index: A

CARL HUBBELL   Pitcher
28 years   Bats Right and Left   Throws Left
1931 Record   Won 14   Lost 12   Earned Runs 2.65
Hubbell played in 36 games in 1931 season

Ladies Free Fridays. Polo Grounds speedway entrance is
10 minutes from New York side of Geo. Washington Bridge.
Send stamped, self-addressed envelope to Polo Grounds
for picture of your favorite player.

**Publisher: New York Giants * Manufacturer: Minden Press Inc., New York, NY
* Type: Black & White * Postmark: Not Used * Value Index: C**

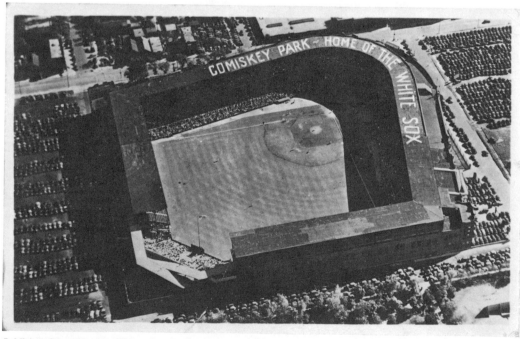

**Publisher: George Burke, Chicago, IL * Manufacturer: George Burke * Type: Real Photgraph * Postmark: Chicago, IL,
February 14, 1940 * Value Index: A**

Lefthander Carl Hubbell pitched his entire 16-year career with the New York Giants and was at his peak from 1933 through 1937. "King Carl" was considered the best pitcher in Baseball, leading the National League in 1933 with 23 wins, 26 wins in 1936, and 27 victories in 1937. The Giants won the Pennant in these years and Hubbell became known as "The Giants Mealticket." Hubbell had pinpoint control and used a screwball with remarkable success. The pitch defies nature and places stress on the elbow. Hubbell twisted his left wrist to the right in releasing the ball to make the ball break down and away from a right-handed hitter. In the 1933 World Series the Giants defeated the Washington Senators four games to one. In the 1936 and 1937 World Series the Giants lost to the Yankees with Hubbell winning one game and losing one game in each Series. In 1934 Hubbell enjoyed the highlight of his career. During the All Star Game played at the Polo Grounds, he faced Babe Ruth, Lou Gehrig, and Jimmy Foxx of the American League All Stars, the three most feared sluggers in Baseball. He proceeded to strike out each of them in 1-2-3 order. He continued the performance in the second inning by striking out Al Simmons and Joe Cronin but then the spell was broken by Bill Dickey's single. Hubbell left the pitching mound after three scoreless innings. Hubbell ended his career with 253 wins and 154 losses.

When the Worlds Fair, known as the Century of Progress, was held in Chicago in 1933, Arch Ward, sports editor of the Chicago Tribune had the idea to feature a Baseball game between the stars of the National and American Leagues. This game would be an excellent method of introducing Baseball to visitors from all over the world. The game was played on July 6, 1933 and one of Baseball's finest showcases was begun. His idea was to include at least one player from each team. Connie Mack of the Philadelphia Athletics was the manager of the American League Team consisting of catcher Rick Farrell, Boston Red Sox; third baseman Jimmy Dykes and outfielder Al Simmons, Chicago White Sox; outfielder Earl Averill, pitchers Wes Farrell and Oral Hildebrand, Cleveland Indians; second Baseman Charley Gehringer, Detroit Tigers; outfielder Ben Chapman, catcher Bill Dickey, first baseman Lou Gehrig, pitcher Lefty Gomez, second baseman Tony Lazzeri, and outfielder Babe Ruth, New York Yankees; first baseman Jimmy Foxx and pitcher Lefty Grove, Philadelphia Athletics; outfielder Stan West, St. Louis Browns; shortstop Joe Cronin and pitcher Alvin Crowder, Washington Senators. John McGraw of the New York Giants was manager of the National League Team which consisted of outfielder Walley Berger, Boston Braves; second baseman Tony Cuccinello, Brooklyn Dodgers; shortstop Woody English, catcher Gabby Hartnett, and pitcher Lon Warneke, Chicago Cubs; outfielder Chick Hafey, Cincinnati Reds; pitcher Carl Hubbell, outfielder Lefty O'Doul, pitcher Hal Schumacher, and first baseman Bill Terry, New York Giants; short-stop Dick Bartell and outfielder Chuck Klein, Philadelphia Phillies; and third baseman Frankie Frisch, pitcher Wild Bill Hallahan, third baseman Pepper Martin, and catcher Jimmie Wilson, St. Louis Cardinals. This photograph shows Comiskey Park during the game that attracted 47,595 fans. The American League won the game by a 4 to 2 score based on Babe Ruth's two-run homer.

Lefty O'Doul may be the finest hitter that did not make it to the Hall of Fame. He began as a pitcher and joined the Yankees in 1919. Appearing in only three games he had a 3.60 ERA with no wins or losses. In 1920 he had a 4.91 ERA. He was sent to the Minors in 1921 and returned to the Yankees in 1922. The Yankees traded him to Boston in 1923 where he won and lost one game compiling a 5.43 ERA. The Red Sox released him to the San Francisco Seals in the Pacific Coast League where he concentrated on hitting and became a success. In 1928 he was the Giants left fielder and had a .319 BA. In 1929 he was traded to the Phillies and led the National League with a .398 BA, 32 HRs, and 122 RBI. In 1932, playing with Brooklyn, O'Doul won his second batting championship

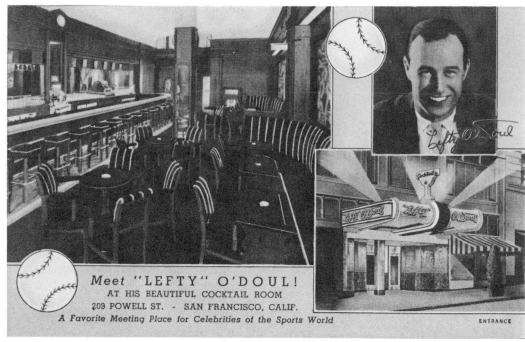

Publisher: Lefty O'Doul's, San Francisco, CA, Card No. 9A-H2081 * Manufacturer: Curt Teich Co., Chicago, IL * Postmark: Not Used * Value Index: A

with a .368 BA. O'Doul was traded to the Giants in the middle of the 1933 season and the Giants won the Pennant and then the World Series against the Washington Senators. Although he had a .349 BA during his seven years as an outfielder he did not qualify as a member of the Hall of Fame.

Fenway Park in Boston was completely refurbished prior to the 1934 season shortly after Tom Yawkee purchased the Red Sox from Bob Quinn. When Fenway Park was built in 1912 the main grandstand was steel and concrete and the bleachers in centerfield were wood. The bleachers were changed to steel and concrete. The Osborn Engineering Company performed the job for the opening on April 17, 1934. The work has remained unaltered to date. Yawkee was able to add the necessary money into the team to buy top players, including a youngster named Ted Williams from San Diego, CA who became one of Baseball's great stars. This photograph shows the "New Fenway Park" shortly after it opened. The distance to the left field wall had been reduced from 318 to 312 feet and the distance along the right field line was increased from 318 to 334

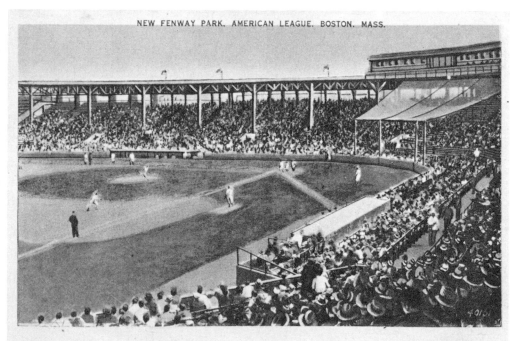

Publisher: United Art Co., Boston, MA, Card No. 40161 * Manufacturer: Metrocraft, Everett, MA * Type: Linen * Postmark: Not Used * Value Index: B

feet. With the new centerfield bleachers the distance was reduced from 468 to 389 feet. The "Green Monster," a concrete wall painted green, replaced the wooden wall and extended from left field to the centerfield bleachers, becoming an inviting target for righthand batters.

This photograph may look familiar to you as it is the same as the scene of Sportsman's Park taken during the 1926 World Series when the Cardinals upset the Yankees. It was extremely popular and was used on Postcards for two decades until after World War II. Sportsman's Park was owned by the American League St. Louis Browns and the National League Cardinals shared the park. Although the Browns usually finished deep in the second division the Cardinals won three Pennants in the 1930s and were World Champions in 1931 and 1934. The Cardinals of the 1930s were known as the "Gas House Gang" and are remembered as some of the best and most colorful players in Baseball history.

Publisher: E.C. Kropp Co., Milwaukee, WI, Card No. 98 * Manufacturer: E.C. Kropp Co. * Type: Pre-Linen * Postmark: Not Used * Value Index: B

Babe Ruth's fame spread beyond the borders of the U.S. as he was also considered a hero in Japan. After his final season with the Yankees in 1934, a team of Major League All Stars, led by Ruth, went to Japan to play four exhibition games against a Japanese All Star Team. The U.S. team was greeted by more than one-half million persons in a huge parade. The first game was played in Tokyo on November 4, 1934 before an overflow crowd of 64,000 fans. The legend on the front of this extremely rare Postcard tells the story. "This is the moment when Babe Ruth, who is called Home Run King of the World, swung hard and hit the ball.

Publisher: Not Indicated * Manufacturer: Not Indicated * Type: Linen * Postmark: Not Used * Value Index: A

It seems the ball flew over the outfield fence and became a home run. The catcher and umpire stood still with surprise in their eyes and the smiling Babe Ruth has a look of pride and satisfaction on his face. The crowd in the stands watched in silent disbelief." Connie Mack, who served as Baseball's goodwill ambassador in charge of this team told a story relating to this HR. "A Japanese General walked 30 miles to present his sword to the first man who made a HR. He didn't seem to think it was possible to hit a ball so far that a batter could make a HR. When Babe Ruth stepped to the plate and hit the ball out of the Park, the General presented his sword to the King of Swat."

Larry MacPhail, general manager of the Cincinnati Reds, in the early 1930s, was a great innovator. He noticed the popularity of Night Baseball in the Minor Leagues and was convinced it would be good for Major League Baseball. The nation was in the Great Depression and Baseball attendance had dropped. MacPhail realized that most working people could only see their favorite teams on weekends and holidays. Cincinnati had finished last in 1934, had the poorest gate attractions, and were in financial difficulties. After pleading with other National League executives MacPhail obtained permission to try seven night games at Crosley Field during the 1935 season. The first night game was scheduled for May 23, 1935 with rain postponing it until May

Publisher: Kraemer Art Co., Cincinnati, OH * Manufacturer: Not Indicated * Type: Linen * Postmark: Not Used * Value Index: A

24. President Franklin D. Roosevelt, at the White House in Washington, DC, pressed a button to light 632 lamps at the Field.

A crowd of 20,422 saw Reds righthander Paul Derringer win a pitching duel with Philadelpia Phillies righthander Joe Bowman by a 2 to 1 score. The experiment with Night Baseball was a huge success. The crowd was more than 10 times the number of people who would have been available for a daytime game. Soon after this game many other fields installed lights and attendance greatly improved.

This photograph of Briggs Stadium shows its appearance in the mid-1930s. You will note that almost all of the men were wearing hats, a tradition during that period. Although the Tigers won the 1934 and 1935 Pennants they did not win the World Series in 1934; however, they did win the Series in 1935. Catcher Mickey Cochrane was in his second season as a player-manager and he led by the example of being a fiery competitor and an inspiration for the team. First baseman Hank Greenberg was the primary power source for the team as he led the American League with 36 HRs, 170 RBI, and a .328 BA. Seven Tiger players had more than a .300 BA including Mickey Cochrane, Hank Greenberg, Charley Gehringer, Gee Walker,

Publisher: Curt Teich, Chicago, IL, Card No. 32,105951 * Manufacturer: Curt Teich * Type: Pre-Linen * Postmark: Detroit, MI, September 16, 1935 * Value Index: B

Peter Fox, Ray Hayworth, and pitcher Schoolboy Rowe. Rowe won 19 and lost 13 games and Tommy Bridges, famous for his curve ball, won 21 games.

The 1935 Detroit Tigers have a special place in the hearts of Detroit Baseball fans because the Tigers gave Detroit their first World Series Championship. The Tigers also won the Pennant in 1907, 1908, 1909, and 1934, but lost the Series. The Greenfield Cafeteria and Coffee Shop was aware of the Tigers' popularity and issued this Postcard to honor the team and attract customers.

TOP ROW : DENNY CARROL , BILLY ROGELL , ELON HOGSETT , Bat Boy JOE ROGGIN , TOMMY BRIDGES
2 ND. ROW : HEINE SCHUBLE , VIC SORRELL , FRANK RIEBER , JOE SULLIVAN , ALVIN CROWDER , GERALD WALKER
3 RD. ROW : CHARLIE GEHRINGER , HUGH SHELLY , MARVIN OWEN , RAY HAYWORTH , SCHOOLBOY ROWE , ELDEN AUKER , H.GREENBERG
4 TH. ROW : PETE FOX , JOJO WHITE , CY PERKINS , MICKEY COCHRANE , DEL BAKER , FLEA CLIFTON , GOOSE GOSLIN

Publisher: Greenfield's Cafeteria and Coffee Shop, Detroit, MI * Manufacturer: Not Indicated * Type: Sepia & White * Postmark: Not Used * Value Index: A

Detroit is the automobile capital of the world and the manufacturers often used the local team to promote their products. The Chrysler Corporation used the 1935 champions to promote their new line of 1936 automobiles. This Postcard was sent to a man in Baltimore, Maryland, with the message, "Hello: Here for the World Series. Lots of excitement and everybody talking about Baseball—and the new Dodge. You'll be seeing it there soon. Detroit says it's the "Beauty Winner" for 1936. Jack." The Postcard was mailed on October 3 while the Tigers were facing the Chicago Cubs in the World Series. On that day, lefthander Tommie Bridges defeated the Cubs by a 8 to 3 score to tie the at one game

Left, front row: Pete Fox, Jo-Jo White, Cy Perkins, Manager Mickey Cochrane, Del Baker, Flea Clifton, Goose Goslin; second row: Charlie Gehringer, Hugh Shelley, Marvin Owen, Ray Hayworth, Schoolboy Rowe, Elden Auker, Hank Greenberg; third row: Heinie Schuble, Vic Sorrell, Frank Reiber, Joe Sullivan, General Alvin Crowder, Gerry Walker; back row: Denny Carroll, trainer, Billy Rogell, Elon Hogsett and Tommy Bridges.

Publisher: Chrysler Corporation, Detroit, MI * Manufacturer: Not Indicated * Type: Black & White * Postmark: Detroit, MI, October 3, 1935 * Value Index: A

apiece. Notice the likeness between this photograph and the one used by the Greenfield Cafeteria and Coffee Shop, except for the fact that the players are wearing caps in this illustration. Also, the batboy Joe Roggin is missing in this photograph. The two photographs must have been taken only seconds apart.

Baseball and its players have been used for advertising purposes since the game began. In 1935 player-manager Mickey Cochrane was in his last season as a full-time player and he led the Detroit Tigers to the World Championship. He was in demand as a spokesman for various products including B.F. Goodrich tires. The same Postcard was widely used as it was printed with the names of many B.F. Goodrich dealers throughout the U.S. to send to their customers.

Publisher: B.F. Goodrich Co. * Manufacturer: Not Indicated * Type: U.S. Government Postal Card * Postmark: Not Used * Value Index: A

With nicknames such as Dizzy (Dean), Daffy (Dean), Ducky (Medwick), Pepper (Martin), Rip (Collins), Lippy (Durocher), Big Cat (Mize), Pop (Haines), and Fordham Flash (Frisch) you would expect the St. Louis Gashouse Gang of the 1930s to be a wild and distinctive bunch of players—and they were. In addition, they won the Pennant and World Series in 1931 and 1934. In 1936, when this Postcard was issued, the Gashouse Gang was intact, but they finished the season in second place, five game behind the Giants.

Despite the fact that they did not win every Pennant and World Series, they were the most colorful team and great crowd pleasers wherever they went. They gave outrageous quotations to media reporters, had their own band,

Publisher: St. Louis Cardinals, St. Louis, MO * Manufacturer: Curt Teich Co., Chicago, IL * Type: Linen * Postmark: Not Used * Value Index: A

and lived a full life. Pepper Martin, Dizzy Dean, Frankie Frisch, Pop Haines, Ducky Medwick, and Johnny Mize all were inducted into the Hall of Fame.

The American League was organized as the second Major League in 1901 and Chicago is the only city to have teams continously in both Leagues. Boston had the Braves in the National League and the Red Sox in the American League until 1952 when the Braves moved to Milwaukee. St. Louis had the Cardinals in the National League and the Browns in the American League until the Browns moved to Baltimore and became the Orioles in 1954. In 1955 the Athletics left Philadelphia for Kansas City leaving the Phillies in the National League as the only team in that area. There were three teams in the New York area until the New York Giants and the Brooklyn Dodgers left to become the San Francisco

Publisher: The J.O. Stoll Co., Chicago, IL, Card No. 7A-H732 * Manufacturer: Curt Teich Co., Chicago, IL * Type: Linen * Postmark: Not Used * Value Index: C

Giants and the Los Angeles Dodgers. Only the Yankees of the American League remained in New York. This photograph shows the two Chicago ball parks as they were in the 1930s. The year 1926 saw extensive renovations to both of them.

This photograph of the Polo Grounds was taken during a World Series, in the late 1930s, from the second deck in left field showing home plate only 278 feet away. The Giants had defeated the Washington Senators in the 1933 World Series and in 1936 the Giants battled the Yankees losing four games to two. Rightfielder Mel Ott led the Giants to the 1936 Pennant with 33 HRs and 135 RBI, while player-manager Bill Terry, then a backup first baseman, proved he remained a dangerous hitter with a .310 BA. In 1937 the Giants again won the Pennant, thanks largely to Ott's 31 HRs and 95 RBI but lost to the Yankees four games to one.

Publisher: Manhattan Postcard Publishing Co., New York, NY, Card No. 75 * Manufacturer: Curt Teich Co., Chicago, IL * Type: Linen * Postmark: Not Used * Value Index: D

Johnny Vander Meer was a left hand fastball pitcher who never won 20 games in a season while in the Major Leagues and ended his 13-year career with 121 losses and 119 wins. However, he will alway be remembered in Baseball history for an important accomplishment. While pitching for the Cincinnati Reds he threw two no-hitters back-to-back, becoming the only Major League pitcher to perform this feat. He was the first Reds' pitcher to have a no-hitter since Hod Eller in 1919. On June 11, 1938 Vander Meer beat the Boston Braves by a 3 to 0 score at Crosley Field without allowing any hits. Four days later, during the first night game under the lights at Ebbets Field in Brooklyn, he was facing the

Publisher: Val Decker Packing Co., Cincinnati, OH * Manufacturer: Orcajo Photo Art, Dayton, OH * Type: Real Photograph * Postmark: Not Used * Value Index: B

Dodgers. Vander Meer was extremely wild that evening although he did not allow a hit for eight innings. Dodger supporters, normally the most loyal fans, were caught in the magnitude of the moment and were actually rooting wildly for the Cincinnati pitcher. With 38,748 screaming fans on their feet, Vander Meer loaded the bases with only one out. He induced Ernie Koy to hit a ground ball to third baseman Lew Riggs, who threw home forcing Goodie Rosen at home plate. Then Leo Durocher hit a fly ball out to centerfield ending the game. There was pandemonium at Ebbets Field as Johnny Vander Meer had pitched his second consecutive no-hitter.

Cleveland was among the first American League cities to play night Baseball. Early in 1939 construction began for light towers to be placed on top of the Municipal Stadium horseshoe shaped rim and the lights were ready for use on June 27. That evening the Indians hosted the Detroit Tigers with "Rapid" Robert Feller pitching against veteran Bobo Newsome. Feller and Cleveland won by a 5 to 0 score as Feller's fast ball was almost unhitable. The Tigers had only one hit; a single by Earl Averill. As interest grew it became obvious that night Baseball was the game of the future for the millions of fans who could come to a game after work.

C-8—Night Baseball at Cleveland Stadium, Cleveland, Ohio

Publisher: George R. Klein News Co., Cleveland, OH, Card No. C-8,3C-H804 * Manufacturer: Curt Teich Co, Chicago, IL * Type: Linen * Postmark: Not Used * Value Index: D

In 1939 the nation celebrated the centennial of Baseball by issuing a postage stamp (shown in the lower left corner of this illustration) acknowledging the 100th anniversary of the game.

The game is considered to have been invented by General Abner Doubleday in Cooperstown although some people have expressed doubt as to his involvement. Cooperstown is the home of the Baseball shrine, the Hall of Fame. The postage stamp attached and cancelled on the picture side of the Postcard shows an unusual view of Ebbets Field. Nearly all other photographs of the stadium show the front entrance. In this view you are looking in from left center field showing the angular construction of the grandstand in this diamond shaped ball park.

Ebbets Field, Brooklyn, N. Y.

Publisher: Herbco Card Co., New York, NY * Manufacturer: Colourpicture Publication, Boston, MA * Type: Linen * Postmark: Brooklyn, NY, June 12, 1939 * Value Index: B

Notice the press box that was not included in the original design which was added in 1929.

The year 1939 was a happy time in the U.S. and for Cincinnati in particular. Baseball was celebrating its centennial year and the U.S. was two years away from World War II. The Reds were in the World Series and this aerial photograph of Crosley Field shows a capacity crowd for one of the World Series games against the Yankees. Bill McKechnie was in his second season as the Reds manager and he was pleased that they had beaten the Cardinals for the Pennant, as the Cardinals had fired him in 1928 after they lost the World Series to the Yankees. The 1939 Reds had a pair of righthanded pitchers, Bucky Walters and Paul Derringer, who had finished first and second in the League with 27 and 25 wins, respectively. The

CROSLEY FIELD, CINCINNATI, OHIO

Publisher: Kraemer Art Co., Cincinnati, OH * Manufacturer: Kraemer Art Co * Type: Linen * Postmark: Brooklyn, NY, August 7, 1940 * Value Index C

Reds lost four consecutive games to the Yankees. Derringer lost the first game by a 2 to 1 score and the other games were 4 to 0, 7 to 3, and 7 to 4. The Reds won the 1940 League Pennant and defeated the Detroit Tigers in the World Series.

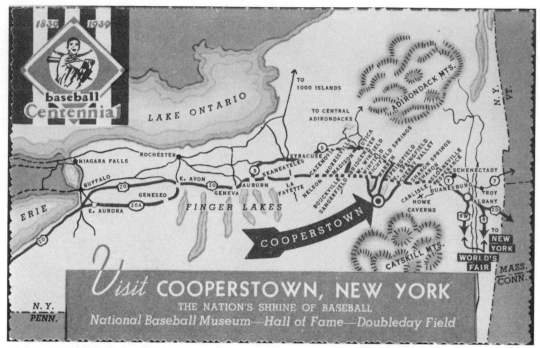

Publisher: National Baseball Museum Hall of Fame, Cooperstown, NY, Card No. 9A-H628 * Manufacturer: Curt Teich Co., Chicago, IL * Type: Linen * Postmark: Not Used * Value Index: B

The town of Cooperstown is the home of the Baseball Hall of Fame. The pastoral setting of the area helps to portray how Baseball evolved in small towns throughout America. On December 30, 1907 a national commission, after a three-year study, accepted Cooperstown as Baseball's birthplace.

They based their conclusion on the testimony of Abner Graves that, in 1839, when he was a young Cooperstown schoolboy he was taught the game by a fellow student named Abner Doubleday who had altered the popular game of Townball. According to Graves, Doubleday used a stick to mark out a diamond shaped field in the dirt, limited the players to nine people per side, added four bases, and used a pitcher and catcher. Those who refuted Doubleday's part in Baseball history indicate that in 1839 he was away at West Point Academy where he graduated in 1842. When Abner Graves died in 1935, a trunk was discovered in his attic containing an old badly worn homemade baseball. The baseball was purchased by Cooperstown resident, Stephen C. Clark, a philanthropist who developed the idea of a museum to house this baseball and other memorabilia associated with the game. Cooperstown decided to have a centennial celebration in 1939 and this rare advertising Postcard shows that all roads lead to Cooperstown.

Catcher Ernie Lombardi played 17 seasons in the National League and is considered one of the finest catchers and one of the slowest men to play Baseball. When he retired at the end of the 1947 season he had compiled a .306 BA with the Dodgers, Reds, Braves, and Giants. Ernie was 6 feet-3 inches tall and weighed 230 pounds. Despite his lack of running speed, he led the National League in 1938 with a .342 BA and in 1942 with a .330 BA. The good-natured giant was a shy man who found the adoration of the crowd to be embarrassing. He became the most popular Cincinnati player since Edd Roush of the 1919 World Champion Reds. His prominent nose led to the nickname "Schnozz" which stayed with him throughout his career. He is remembered as a outstanding handler of pitchers and having had an excellent throwing arm.

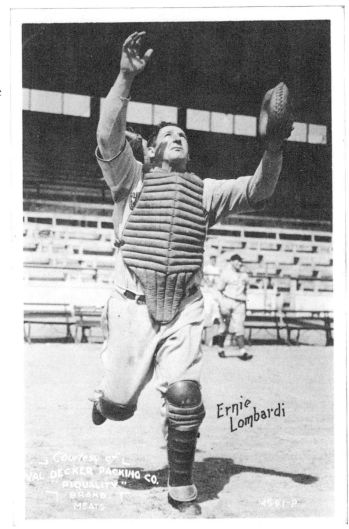

Publisher: Val Decker Packing Co., Card No. 4591-2 * Manufacturer: Obcajo Photo Art, Dayton, OH * Type: Real Photograph * Postmark: Not Used * Value Index: B

In 1931 Paul Derringer burst on the Major League scene with the St. Louis Cardinals and the pitcher had an immediate impact. The tall rookie won 18 and lost 8 games and played a key role in winning the Pennant. He had rookie jitters in the World Series, losing his two starts against the Philadelphia Athletics. The Cardinals rallied to win the Series four games to three. In 1932 he lost 14 and won 11 games and in 1933 he lost the first 2 games and was traded to the Cincinnati Reds. His efforts were not successful and he lost 25 and won 7 games. Many of his defeats were only by one or two runs. In 1934 he won 15 and lost 21 games. As the Reds began to climb out of last place he improved, and in 1936 he won 22 and lost 13 games while the Reds were in sixth place. In 1939 the Reds won their first Pennant in 20 years and he won 25 and lost 7 games. In 1940 the Reds again won the Pennant and Derringer won 20 and lost 12 games. They won the World Series against the Detroit Tigers as Derringer won the 7th game and the Reds and Derringer were at the top of the Baseball world.

Publisher: Val Decker Packing * Manufacturer: Orcajo Photo Art * Type: Real Photograph * Postmark: Not Used * Value Index: C

Baseball has had tragedies over the years, but few were more surprising than the 1940 suicide of Willard Hershberger, the backup catcher to Ernie Lombardi with the Cincinnati Reds. Late in July the Reds were on the way to a Pennant. They were playing the Giants at the Polo Grounds and the Reds had a 4 to 1 lead in the bottom of the ninth inning. The bases were loaded and Harry Danning blasted a grand slam HR and the Giants had a 5 to 4 victory. Hershberger was catching and took the blame by calling for the wrong pitch. His teammates tried to console him but Hershberger became very disconsolate. Two days later, the Reds were playing a doubleheader with the Braves in Boston. Hershberger caught the second game and he had no hits in five times at bat and he failed to field a bunt a few feet from home plate. Manager Bill McKechnie rushed out to Hershberger to find out what was wrong and was told he would discuss it later. McKechnie took him out to dinner and was amazed when he was told that Hershberger was contemplating suicide. McKechnie tried to convince his catcher that he had the best years of his life ahead of him and seemed to have agreement from Hershberger. When Hershberger did not arrive for the doubleheader to be played the next day against the Braves, McKechnie sent someone to the hotel and Hershberger's lifeless body was found with his throat slit by a razor blade. At 29 years of age he had been popular with his teammates and in only three seasons his .316 BA, if extended over a longer period of time, would have been a consideration for the Hall of Fame.

Publisher: Val Decker Packing * Manufacturer: Orcajo Photo Art, Dayton, OH * Type: Real Photograph * Postmark: Not Used * Value Index: C

When the Cincinnati Reds won their second consecutive National League Pennant in 1940, first baseman Frank McCormick provided most of the important hitting with 127 RBI, a .309 BA, and the Most Valuable Player Award. At 6 feet-4 inches tall and 205 pounds McCormick was a spectacular defensive first baseman and so agile that he played second base four times. McCormick had a better season in 1939 with a .332 BA and 128 RBI. He lost the Most Valuable Player Award to his teammate lefthand pitcher Bucky Walters who won 27 games. McCormick played 10 seasons with the Reds, was traded to the Phillies in 1946, and to the Braves in 1947. The Braves won the Pennant in 1948.

Publisher: Val Decker Packing * Manufacturer: Orcajo Photo Art * Type: Real Photograph * Postmark: Not Used * Value Index: C

When Stephen C. Clark initially approached the Baseball hierarchy about a Baseball museum in Cooperstown, New York, National League President Ford Frick was particularly enthusiastic. He obtained the backing of Baseball Commissioner Kenesaw Mountain Landis and American League President Will Harridge and plans were developed for a museum and Hall of Fame honoring the outstanding players in Baseball. A Hall of Fame Committee was organized in conjunction with the Baseball Writers of America. Their first elections were held in 1936. The first five players elected were Ty Cobb, Babe Ruth, Honus Wagner, Christy Mathewson, and Walter Johnson. The rules for election were that a player had to receive 75 percent of the

Doubleday Field, Cooperstown, N. Y., Cavalcade of Baseball, June 12, 1939—2

Publisher: C.W. Hughes & Co.,Inc., Mechanicville, NY, Card No. 0B-H792 * Type: Linen * Postmark: Not Used * Value Index: C

votes cast. Ty Cobb received the most votes, 222 of 225 votes cast, Babe Ruth and Honus Wagner each received 215 votes, Christy Mathewson received 205 votes, and Walter Johnson received 189 votes. The next year included Napoleon LaJoie, Tris Speaker, and Cy Young. In 1938 Grover Cleveland Alexander and in 1939 George Sisler, Eddie Collins, and Willie Keeler were elected. The first induction ceremony occurred on June 12, 1939 and all were present except Willie Keeler, who had died in 1923, The ceremony was a spectacular event. Following the induction of the original 12 players the membership in the Hall of Fame has had steady growth over the years.

When this Postcard was mailed in 1940 the Detroit Tigers were on their way to a Pennant. The photograph shows an afternoon crowd of fans watching the Tigers in action. The Tigers were the last American League team to install lights in their stadium as Detroit was in an unusual work situation when compared to other cities. The Detroit automotive industry had many people working the night shift and they were able to attend Baseball games during the day. Lights were finally installed in 1948. The view was taken looking from the left field foul line into the right field seats which were located 315 feet from home plate.

677:—BRIGGS STADIUM. DETROIT BASEBALL PARK. DETROIT. MICH.

Publisher: United News Co., Detroit, MI, Card No. 677,43061 * Manufacturer: Metrocraft, Everett, MA * Type: Linen *
Postmark: Detroit, MI, May 5, 1940 * Value Index: C

Ted Williams had many nicknames: "The Splendid Splinter," "The Thumper," and "The Kid." The nickname most fitting to him, "Teddy Ballgame" he gave to himself. Williams unquestionably he was the greatest natural hitter in the last 50 years and was a student of the game. He studied the opposing pitchers more closely than did any other player and as a result he was Baseball's last .400 hitter with a .406 BA in 1941. His lifetime .344 BA was the fifth best in Baseball history. As good as Williams played he frequently became the target of booing fans for not being better. He was annoyed by the comments and showed his displeasure by spitting in the direction of the fans thereby causing more booing. In his later years he made peace with the fans and himself. In his autobiography, *MY TURN AT BAT*, Williams discussed his love-hate relationship with the fans. " I am sure of one thing, I would never spit at those fans again. Boston fans were the best. I was, in the final analysis, the darling of the fans of Boston. From the earliest days, I was their guy, because I was exuberant, I was natural, I was different. I am sorry I was late finding out, but I'm glad I did find it out."

Considering the fact that Williams missed almost five years of his career in World War II and Korea, his record is remarkable. When he left in 1943 he had won two consecutive American League batting titles with a .406 BA in 1941 and .356 BA in 1942. He was home run leader for the two years with 37 HRs and 36 HRs respectively. Ted had 521 career HRs including a HR in his last game and his last time at bat in 1960. The 42-year old Williams had a .316 BA and 29 HRs during that final season.

Publisher: Not Indicated * Manufacturer: Not Indicated * Type: Black & White * Postmark: Not Used * Value Index: B

Over the years the Chicago Cubs have been adopted by many fans who did not live near Chicago. Perhaps the years of frustrating finishes, often in the second division, have rallied so many Baseball fans to the Cub cause. Remembering their past greatness, these fans may be hoping for a revival of those achievements. This photograph shows the Cubs in their last Pennant-winning season in 1945.

CHICAGO NATIONAL LEAGUE BASEBALL CLUB

OUR CUBS IN 1945

Publisher: Grogan Photo Co., Danville, IL * Manufacturer: Grogan Photo Co., Danville, IL * Type: Real Photograph * Postmark: Not Used * Value Index: B

Wrigley Field in Chicago has been described as the most beautiful stadium in Baseball. The Wrigley family, which owned the team for 60 years, took particular care to make the stadium as attractive as possible. Ivy grows on the outfield brick wall which encircles the entire field. Occasionally the ivy causes problems such as during the 1945 World Series when Andy Pafko, Cubs left fielder, had trouble finding the ball hit by the Tigers Roy Cullenbine when it lodged in the ivy vines. This photograph taken in the 1940s shows the final seating renovations made primarily in the centerfield bleacher section. The legend on the back of the Postcard states, "Wrigley Field America's Finest Recreation Center. Everything for your convenience and comfort. Attractive Restaurants. Modern Bleachers. Comfortable Seats. Home of the Chicago Cubs." This ball park houses Baseball's first permanent concession stand installed by the Chicago Whales of the Federal League when the park opened in 1914. When the Federal League disbanded after the 1915 season the Cubs took over the park and continue to use it.

Beautiful WRIGLEY FIELD . . . Home of the Chicago Cubs

Publisher: Chicago Cubs, Chicago, IL * Manufacturer: Curt Teich, Chicago, IL * Type: Linen * Postmark: Sikeston, MO, March 15, 1942 * Value Index: B

This view is what the fans would see during the 1942 World Series from the second deck of the right field seats at Yankee Stadium. This was the 20th season of the historic ball park and, as usual, the Yankees had won the Pennant. Beginning in their new home in 1923 the Yankees won the Pennant in 1923, 1926, 1927, 1928, 1932, 1936, 1937, 1938, 1939, and 1941. Also, in all those years except for 1926, when they lost to the St. Louis Cardinals, the Yankees won every World Championship. Although 1942 was the first full year of World War II, the Yankees had most of their key players during that year. Second baseman Joe Gordon had a .322 BA, highest on the team with 18 HRs and 103 RBI. The Yankee Clipper Joe DiMaggio had a .305 BA, 21 HRs, and led the team with 114 RBI. Charley Keller was the team leader with 26 HRs and was second to DiMaggio with 108 RBI. Although the Yankees won the Pennant by 9 games and were known as the "Bronx Bombers" the Cardinals were not awed by the Yankee reputation for hitting and won the World Series four games to one.

Publisher: Interborough News Co., New York, NY, Card No. 136,7A-H2099 * Manufacturer: Curt Teich, Chicago, IL * Type: Linen * Postmark: Flushing, NY, August 20, 1942 * Value Index: E

The St. Louis Cardinal's fans cheered the 1942 National League Pennant winners in Sportsman's Park, owned by the St. Louis Browns. The Browns built the stadium in 1909 and invited the Cardinals to share the facilities in 1920 after the Cardinals were forced to abandon Robison Field. This Postcard was used in 1942 as the Cardinals were battling for another Pennant. However, the publisher has continued to use a photograph taken during the 1926 World Series. The view was a popular scene, as it was used until 1944.

Publisher: E.C. Kropp Co., Milwaukee, WI, Card No. 98,4369 * Manufacturer: E.C. Kropp Co., Milwaukee, WI * Type: Linen * Postmark: St. Louis, MO, June 22, 1942 * Value Index: D

Lefthander Joe Nuxhall had a fine pitching career, winning 135 Major League games in 16 seasons, most of the games with the Cincinnati Reds. His place in Baseball history is not as much for his accomplishments on the pitching mound as it is for the fact that he was the youngest player to appear in a Major League game. The situation was unique, as teams were desperate for talent during World War II because many of the top stars were in military service. In 1944 a 15-year-old schoolboy, pitcher Joe Nuxhall, was becoming known in Hamilton, Ohio. The Cincinnati Reds signed him to a contract on June 10, more than one month before his birthday. On July 30 he completed a game between the Reds and the Cardinals. The nervous youngster recorded the final two outs, but, unfortunately before doing so, he gave up 5 runs, 5 walks, and 2 hits. Everyone realized he was not ready for the big leagues. When he overcame his wildness and displayed the same tenacity that made him an all-star football, basketball, and baseball player he was returned to the Reds in 1952. His playing career ended in 1966 and he retired to the Reds broadcasting booth where he is today as play-by-play announcer. His place as the youngest player in Major Leagues history will probably remain forever.

Publisher: Cincinnati Reds, Cincinnati, OH * Manufacturer: Not Indicated * Type: Black & White * Postmark: Not Used * Value Index: C

Joe Nuxhall—Cincinnati Redlegs

The most famous and probably the best of the brothers playing Baseball were the DiMaggios. They grew up near the San Francisco waterfront and it was not surprising that they parlayed their fame and money into a popular restaurant on Fisherman's Wharf. Vince, the eldest of the brothers was the least successful player. He played for 10 years in the National League with Boston, Cincinnati, Pittsburgh, Philadelphia, and New York. He had a .249 BA and led the National League in strike-outs during 6 of the 10 years. His .289 BA in 1940 was the highest average that he earned during those years. Dom, the youngest brother, had the misfortune to play in Joe's shadow. Dom's entire 11-year career was with

Publisher: Joe DiMaggio's Restaurant, San Francisco, CA * Manufacturer: Curt Teich, Chicago, IL * Type: Linen * Postmark: Not Used * Value Index: B

the Boston Red Sox, where he was considered the second-best centerfielder in the American League, with Joe being the best. Although the Red Sox and Yankees frequently battled for the Pennant, usually Joe and the Yankees would win. Dom, nicknamed "The Little Professor" because of his scholarly appearance had a .298 BA. His best season was 1950 when he had a .328 BA, leading the League with 131 RBI and 15 stolen bases. In 13 seasons Joe compiled a .325 BA and led the League with a .381 BA in 1939 and a .352 BA in 1940. He also led the League with 125 RBI in 1941 and 155 RBI in 1948. Joe was elected to the Hall of Fame in 1955.

This photograph shows Wrigley Field in 1945 as the Chicago Cubs won the first Pennant since 1938. At the beginning of the season the hopes for a Pennant were not too high. The Cubs had basically the same team as in 1944, when they completed the season 30 games behind the Pennant-winning Cardinals. Cubs Manager Charley Grimm skillfully guided them. First baseman Phil Caveretta had a .355 BA to lead the League. Third baseman Stan Hack had a .323 BA, second baseman Don Johnson had a .302 BA, and centerfielder Andy Pafko posted a .298 BA and 110 RBI. Pitcher Hank Wyse had his best season with 22 wins and 10 losses. Perhaps the real key to the Cub victory was the acquisition of

Publisher: Not Indicated, Card No. 283 * Manufacturer: AC Co., Chicago, IL * Type: Chrome * Postmark: Chicago, IL, September 30, 1945 * Value Index: D

Hank Borowy from the New York Yankees at midseason for $100,000. Borowy became one of the best righthanded pitchers in the National League, winning 11 and losing 2 games with a 2.13 ERA. Righthanded pitchers Claude Passeau and Paul Derringer each won 17 and lost 16 games. Derringer, a former star with the Cincinnati Reds, regained his form after 7 wins and 13 losses with the Cubs in 1944. With all of the pieces fitting together the Cubs won 98 and lost 56 games to finish three games in front of the Cardinals who had won the Pennant for the previous 3 years.

This photograph shows Briggs Stadium in 1945 devoid of lights. Although night Baseball was begun in 1934, Detroit did not have lights until 1948. The Detroit fans had other thoughts in mind: they were hoping the Tigers would win the American League Pennant. In 1944 they were only one game behind the Browns, who won their only Pennant. World War II was coming to an end and the various Baseball players were being released from military service. Hank Greenberg, the most feared slugger in Baseball, returned to play with Detroit. In less than one-half of the season he had 13 HRs and 60 RBI, enabling the Tigers to win the Pennant by 1-1/2 games over Washington. Lefthander Hal Newhouser pitched brilliantly, winning 25

Publisher: United News Co., Detroit, MI, Card No. 235,3B-H788 * Manufacturer: Curt Teich, Chicago, IL * Type: Linen * Postmark: Detroit, MI, March 14, 1945 * Value Index: D

and losing 9 games to lead the American League. They played the Chicago Cubs in the World Series, and won four games to three, and Newhouser won the last game by a 9 to 3 score.

Sportsman's Park was dressed in World Series finery four times during the 1940s. The Cardinals won the Pennant in 1942, 1943, 1944, and 1946. The Browns who owned the ball park won their only American League Pennant in 1944. This photograph, taken during a 1940s World Series game, shows the bunting proudly hanging from the facade of the second deck. The view shows the first base line and was only the second photograph of this scene to be published as a Postcard since 1926. The Cardinals had a multitude of stars in the 1940s including an outfielder "Stan The Man" Musial who joined the team in 1941. He was the best player and the favorite of the fans. He was in only 12 games during the season and had a .426 BA, and 20 hits in 47 times at bat. He

Sportsman's Park, Home of the St. Louis Cardinals and Browns, St. Louis, Mo. 141

Publisher: Paul Monroe Co., St. Louis, MO, Card No. 141,63712 * Manufacturer: Tichnor Bros. Inc., Boston, MA * Type: Linen * Postmark: St. Louis, MO, February 17, 1945 * Value Index: D

stayed with the Cardinals for 22 years, had a lifetime .331 BA, and won seven National League batting titles. Rightfielder Enos "Country" Slaughter joined Musial in the Baseball Hall of Fame. Other important players included centerfielder Terry Moore, shortstop Marty Marion, and righthander Mort Cooper who was the ace of the pitching staff, winning 22 games in 1942, 21 games in 1943, and 22 games in 1944. His brother Walker Cooper was one of the best catchers in Baseball. In 1944 the Browns finished one game in front of Detroit as shortstop Vern Stephens led the way with 20 HRs and a league leading 109 RBI. Outfielders Mike Krevich .301 BA and Al Zarilla .299 BA had the highest BAs on the team. Nelson Potter with 19 wins and Jack Kramer with 17 wins were the leading pitchers. The Browns lost their only World Series to the Cardinals four games to two.

New York's Yankee Stadium is the only Baseball stadium depicted on a breakfast cereal box. During World War II people were encouraged to write letters to service people overseas. The Kellogg Company decided to do its part to aid this effort by placing famous American scenes on their cereal boxes. These scenes were intended to be cut out, folded, and mailed. There was room for a message on the inside and back of the folded Postcard. Among other known Kellogg Postcards are the Washington Monument in Washington, DC and the Empire State Building in New York City.

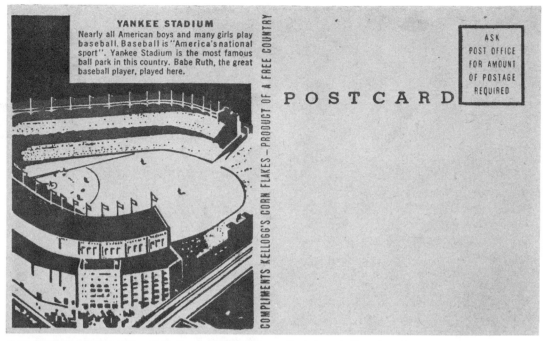

Publisher: Kellogg's Corn Flakes, Battle Creek, MI * Manufacturer: Not Indicated * Type: Red, Green & White * Postmark: Not Used * Value Index: A

During the 1940s, when this Postcard was produced, the New York Giants did not win a National League Pennant. However, in 1947 they had one of the hardest hitting lineups in Baseball history. The Giants led the League with 211 HRs versus the Pittsburgh Pirates' 156 HRs. First baseman Johnny Mize with 51 HRs shared the League lead with Pittsburgh's Ralph Kiner. Four of the League's first five HR hitters were Giants, rightfielder Willard Marshall was third with 36 HRs, catcher Walker Cooper was fourth with 35 HRs, and centerfielder Bobby Thomson fifth with 29 HRs. Despite this overwhelming power the Giants finished in fourth place, 13 games behind the Pennant-winning Dodgers. The Giants also led the League in 1948 with 164 HRs.

Publisher: Herbco Card Co., New York, NY, Card No. 109, K2035 * Manufacturer: Colourpicture Publication, Boston, MA * Type: Linen * Postmark: Brooklyn, NY, September 30, 1949 * Value Index: D

Mize had 40 HRs to share the HR title with Kiner and the Giants finished in fifth place. This photograph was taken from right center field and shows how the stands were an inviting target for HR hitters. Although the center field bleachers were 475 feet from home plate, the right and left field foul lines were only 258 feet and 280 feet respectively. These distances presented easy targets for the Giants of 1947 and 1948. When this Postcard was mailed in 1949, the Giants were second to the Pennant-winning Dodgers with 147 HRs, compared to the Dodgers' 152 HRs. They were in fifth place in the League standings.

Publisher: Pittsburgh Pirates, Pittsburgh, PA * Manufacturer: Photo by
Jacino * Type: Black & White * Postmark: Pittsburgh, PA, September 19, 1949
* Value Index: B

Sportsman's Park, St. Louis, Missouri

Publisher: Gibson Merchandise Co., St. Louis, MO, Card No. K1430 * Manufacturer: Colourpicture Publications, Boston,
MA * Type: Linen * Postmark: St. Louis, MO, July 5, 1948, Value Index: D

Outfielder Ralph Kiner had a relatively brief Major League career beginning in 1946 when he joined the Pittsburgh Pirates. He was the greatest HR hitter in the National League leading the League from his first season for seven consecutive years. In 1946 he hit 23 HRs as a rookie. In 1947 he hit 51 HRs, had 127 RBI, and a .313 BA. Considering the fact that the Pirates finished in last place Kiner's statistics are very impressive. Kiner said later, "The hardest thing in the world is to play for a losing team. I always had a strong competitive drive and I hated to lose." His best season was 1949 with 54 HRs, 127 RBI, and a 310 BA. Despite his success in 1949 the Pirates finished sixth in the League with 71 wins and 83 losses. During 1950, 1951, and 1952 he had 47, 42, and 37 HRs. A chronic back ailment shortened his career, which ended in 1955 while he was with the Cleveland Indians. During the 10 seasons he hit 369 HRs which is equal to one HR for every 7.1 times at bat. Only Babe Ruth had a higher HR percentage. Ralph Kiner became a Baseball broadcaster for the New York Mets in 1961 and continues in that assignment. He was elected to the Hall of Fame in 1975.

This aerial view of Sportsman's Park in St. Louis was taken during the 1946 World Series between the St. Louis Cardinals and the Boston Red Sox. The Series is considered one of the most exciting as the teams fought to the last inning of the seventh game. The Red Sox won the first game at Sportsman's Park by a 3 to 2 score. The second game featured Harry "The Cat" Brecheen pitching a 4-hit shutout and a 3 to 0 victory. At Boston, the 25-game winner, righthander Boo Ferriss, shut out the Cardinals by 6 hits with a 4 to 0 score. The Cardinals pounded Boston's Tex Hughson and five relief pitchers for 20 hits, the game ending with a 12 to 3 score and the fifth game was won by the Red sox with a 6 to 3 score. Back at Sportsman's Park Harry Brecheen evened the Series by allowing only seven hits for a 4 to 1 win. During the seventh game a standing-room-only crowd of 36,143 fans saw the Red Sox take a 1 to 0 lead in the first inning then the Cardinals tied it in the second inning. In the fifth inning the Cardinals scored twice for a 3 to 1 lead and Boston tied the score in the eighth inning. In the bottom of the eighth inning Cardinal rightfielder Enos Slaughter had a hit a single off relief pitcher Bob Klinger. Klinger retired the next two batters and Harry Walker hit a double to Centerfield. Slaughter began running at the crack of the bat and was expected to stop at third base. However, without slowing his pace he raced to home plate with the winning run. Sportsman's Park erupted with a wild and enthusiastic celebration by the fans.

This scene occurred on May 28, 1946 when the New York Yankees played their first night game at Yankee Stadium. Until that time Yankee owner Colonel Jacob Ruppert and his general manager Ed Barrow were strongly opposed to night Baseball. They stated that it was beneath the dignity of Baseball's most powerful team to use lights to attract fans when they were attracting large numbers of fans without the use of lights. When the Yankees were sold by the Ruppert family to a triumvirate of Larry MacPhail, Del Webb, and Dan Topping their first action was to install lights. Larry MacPhail had pioneered night Baseball at Cincinnati in 1935 and at Brooklyn in 1938. Installing the lights proved to be correct for the Yankees as they had more than 2,000,000 fans,

Publisher: Acacia Card Co., New York, NY, Card No. 169,79635 * Manufacturer: Not Indicated * Type: Linen * Postmark: Brooklyn, NY, October 19, 1949 * Value Index: D

beginning in 1946, for five consecutive years and they were the first team to reach that attendance record. The only negative aspect for the Yankees was the fact they lost the first game under the lights to the Washington Senators by a 2 to 1 score.

Night Baseball began in the National League in 1934 when Larry MacPhail installed lights in Crosley Field. In 1939, Connie Mack installed lights at Shibe Park as Philadelphia became the first American League team to do so. The Detroit Tigers were the last American League team to install lights by waiting until 1948. The reasoning for this late installation was that the three-shift automobile workers did not require lights at the games. The large number of workers on the night shift were available during the daylight hours to attend the games. Owner Walter Briggs finally bowed to the inevitable by installing lights. This photograph was taken during the first night game at Briggs Stadium on June 15, 1948.

Briggs Stadium, Detroit, Mich.   21

Publisher: Arcadia Greeting Card Co., Detroit, MI, Card No. 21K2756 * Manufacturer: Colour Picture Publications, Boston, MA * Type: Linen * Postmark: Not Used * Value Index: B

The impact of Jackie Robinson on Baseball has been thoroughly documented. When he joined the Brooklyn Dodgers in 1947 he was the first Negro (as a Black or Afro-American was designated at that time) to play in the Major Leagues since the turn of the century. Two Negro brothers, Moses Fleetwood Walker and Welday Walker played briefly with Toledo of the American Association in 1884. However, their careers lasted less than a season because of strong objections from the white players. After the integration of World War II and the Black insistence for equality, General Manager Branch Rickey of the Brooklyn Dodgers sensed a change coming and he decided to break the color line in Baseball. He knew the first Black would be subjected to initial abuse and he wanted someone who could withstand that abuse. He selected Jackie Robinson, a four-sport star at UCLA and a Lieutenant in the U.S. Army during World War II. Robinson was playing shortstop for the Kansas City Monarchs of the Negro National League when he met Rickey at his office. The Dodger manager asked many tough questions including how would Robinson react if someone hit him. " Mr. Rickey, do you want a ball player who's afraid to fight back?" Robinson asked. Rickey said, "I want a ball player with guts enough not to fight back. You've got to do this job with base hits and stolen bases and by fielding ground balls, Jackie, and nothing more." And he did. Robinson signed a Dodger contract in 1946 and played with the Montreal Royals of the International League where he was an instant success leading the League with a .349 BA. In 1947 he joined the Dodgers, becoming a star and leading the League with 29 stolen bases and a .297 BA. In 1949 his .342 BA gave him the League title. He retired in 1956 with a career .311 BA.

Sincerely yours,
Jackie Robinson

Publisher: Not Indicated * Manufacturer: Not Indicated * Type: Real Photograph * Postmark: Not Used * Value Index: A

When Bob Feller left a Van Meter, Iowa farm in 1936 to join the Cleveland Indians he was a legend because of his blazing fast- ball. He was called "Rapid Robert" in high school. Feller made his debut on July 6, 1936 against the Cardinals in an exhibition game. During three innings he struck out eight Cardinal batters. As Feller recalled in his autobiography STRIKEOUT STORY, Cardinal pitcher Dizzy Dean, with an outstanding fastball of his own, was impressed. When the photographers asked Dean to pose with Feller Dean replied, "If it's all right with him, it's all right with me." Despite losing four seasons during World War II, when he was in his prime, Feller won 266 games during his 18-year career. He also had 2,581 career strikeouts including 348 strikeouts in 1946. Feller had 3 no-hitters and a record of 12 one-hitters before entering the Hall of Fame in 1962. The Postcards of the Cleveland Indians were available at the time by writing to Cleveland broadcaster Van Patrick and this illustration shows Feller ready to throw one of his 100-mile-an-hour fastballs.

Publisher: Van Patrick, Cleveland, OH * Manufacturer: Not Indicated * Type: Real Photograph * Postmark: Not Used * Value Index: B

Sometimes the message written on the back of a Postcard is as interesting as the view shown on the Postcard itself. A lady in Cleveland, Ohio wrote to a friend in Kansas City, Missouri, "I'm listening to a ball game being played at the Stadium. Cleveland—Philadelphia Wish I was there." As the lady indicated many people were caught up in baseball fever during the Summer of 1948 and when Cleveland fans could not go to the stadium they followed the events by listening to Jack Graney and Jimmy Dudley on the radio. This photograph, taken directly above Municipal Stadium, indicates the record crowds that attended the games during that period.

C-26—Municipal Stadium, Cleveland, Ohio

Publisher: George R. Klein News Co., Cleveland, OH, Card No. C-26,4B-H1241 * Manufacturer: Curt Teich Co., Chicago, IL * Type: Linen * Postmark: Warrensville, OH, May 22, 1948 * Value Index: E

When the season was over 2,620,627 fans had attended the Indians' 77 home games. This attendance record remained for almost 30 years until broken by the Los Angles Dodgers.

"Spahn and Sain and Pray for Rain" was the battle cry of the 1948 Boston Braves as they fought for their first National League Pennant since 1914. Their hopes were on the pitching of lefthander Warren Spahn and righthander Johnny Sain. Spahn contributed 15 victories to the winning of the Pennant and completed his career with 363 wins. A total that is more than any lefthander in Baseball history. Sain had 24 wins with a 2.60 ERA in 1948. Although the battle cry was a clever way of indicating that the Braves had a two-man pitching staff, it was not true. Rookie righthander Vern Bickford was a surprise with his 11 wins and 5 losses. When the 1948 season was over the Braves had 91 wins and a 6-1/2-game lead over the Cardinals. The Braves had an abundance of good hitters; however, Cleveland pitching stopped the Braves in the World Series and the Indians won the Series in 6 games.

Boston Braves Baseball Team of 1948

Front L. to R.—Sibby Sisti, Clyde Shoun, Bob Keely, Fred Fitzsimmons, Billy Southworth, Johnny Cooney, Bob Elliott, Red Barrett, Bill Salkeld, Vern Bickford, Phil Masi, Jim Russell.
Second L. to R.—George Young, Frank McCormick, Ernie White, Connie Ryan, John Sain, Bob Hogue, Mike McCormick, Clint Conatser, Jeff Heath, John Antonelli, Warren Spahn, Nelson Potter.
Third L. to R.—Bob Sturgeon, Si Johnson, Earl Torgeson, Al Dark, Tommy Holmes, Bill Voiselle, John Beazley, Al Lyons.
Bat Boys L. to R.—Charlie Chronopoulos, Tom Ferguson, Frank McNulty.

Publisher:Tichnor Bros.,Inc., Boston, MA, Card No. 78732 * Manufacturer: Tichnor Bros., Inc. * Type: Linen * Postmark: Not Used * Value Index: C

Larry Doby did not receive the same fanfare as Jackie Robinson. He quietly broke the color line with the Cleveland Indians in 1947. He was the American League's first Negro ball player. Cleveland owner Bill Veeck purchased Doby from the Newark Eagles of the Negro National League in 1947 and immediately brought him to the Indians. Doby had played college basketball and Baseball on predominately white teams before joining the Indians. Player-manager Lou Boudreau recalled Doby's first appearance, "We talked for quite awhile and I told Larry exactly what my plans were for him. I pointed out that because he was the first player of his race to enter the American League, he was bound to be the subject of a great deal of newspaper publicity, and I also thought it would be a good bet he would be reading stories saying I would be prejudiced in my dealings with him. I made it plain that he should pay no attention to such sensationalism and just concentrate on the job of playing ball as well as he knew how." Obviously nervous and under pressure, Doby's initial efforts were not impressive. He played in 29 games with 32 times at bat and a .156 BA. Boudreau proposed playing Doby slowly. "Because the pressure on him was tremendous and I was unwilling to let one-half year's playing under such terrific odds spoil his future. I tried to spot him where I thought he would be most likely to come through. In that way, I hoped to assist Larry in gaining the confidence he had to have before he made good in our League." Boudreau's handling of Doby paid dividends. In 1948 his .301 BA, 14 HRs, and 66 RBI were important in the Indians winning the Pennant. He compiled a 13-year .283 BA. His initial position was second base, but he achieved his greatest success as an outfielder.

Publisher: Cleveland Indians, Cleveland, OH * Manufacturer: Not Indicated * Type: Real Photograph * Postmark: Not Used * Value Index: B

The influx of former Major League players into the radio and television broadcasting booths has been well documented. In the 1990s more than one-half of the people who broadcast Major League Baseball were former players. The first player to make league broadcasting his second career was Jack Graney, from Cleveland, who moved behind the microphone for the Indians in 1932 and was also the first ex-player to broadcast a World Series. His broadcasting career continued until he retired in 1953. Jack Graney had a colorful broadcast style and was one of the first announcers to include the sponsor's name into his play-by-play commentary. For example, "The centerfielder's riding the Red Wing (Mobil Gasoline Trademark) back for a fly ball. He got it." This slightly oversized photograph and Postcard promoted the Indians' broadcasts over the Standard Network of six Ohio radio stations. Graney is seated second from the right and his broadcasting partner is seated to Graney's left.

Publisher: Standard Baseball Family, Cleveland, OH * Manufacturer: Not Indicated * Type: Black & White * Postmark: Not Used * Value Index: A

When Lou Boudreau was the player-manager of the Cleveland Indians in the 1940's he led by example. His leadership reached its pinnacle in 1948 when the Tribe won the Pennant in a dramatic one-game playoff with the Boston Red Sox and then the World Series against the Boston Braves. Boudreau was fortunate to enjoy a year that many players dream about but very few achieve. He had a .355 BA, 106 RBI, fielded brilliantly at shortstop, and seemed to make all of the correct managerial decisions. He was winner of the American League Most Valuable Player Award for 1948. He documented this amazing season in his autobiography, PLAYER MANAGER. Fans could purchase his book by using this Postcard as an order form to the publisher. He remained with the Tribe through 1950, and later managed the Boston Red Sox, Kansas City Athletics, and Chicago Cubs. He was elected to the Hall of Fame in 1970.

Player - Manager
By *LOU BOUDREAU*
with
ED FITZGERALD

A Great Baseball Success Story told in the words of the man who lived it.

Please send me .... copies of PLAYER-MANAGER at $2.75 each.

☐ Charge my account. ☐ Cash enclosed.
Add any city or state tax

Name ....

Address ....

Publisher: Burrows, Cleveland, OH * Manufacturer: Not Indicated * Type: Business Reply Card * Postmark: Not Used * Value Index: A

When the Cleveland Indians played the Boston Braves in the 1948 World Series all previous Series attendance records were broken. This aerial photograph shows Municipal Stadium on October 10, 1948 when 86,288 fans packed the huge stadium on the shore of Lake Erie. The legend on this Postcard states that Municipal Stadium had a seating capacity of 85,000; however, there are many fans standing behind the outfield fences. The Cleveland fans were hopeful that Bob Feller would win the Series because, on this date, the Indians were leading three games to one, but the Braves broke a tie score in the seventh inning by scoring 6 runs against Feller and four relief pitchers. The majority of the fans went

Publisher: Klein News Co., Cleveland, OH, Card No. C-26 * Manufacturer: Curt Teich, Chicago, IL * Type: Linen * Postmark: Not Used * Value Index: D

home unhappy; however, the Indians won the Series after the next game in Boston. This photograph continues in use today on one of the Postcards for the stadium.

When this Postcard was issued in 1949 the legend on the back states "Home of the Boston Braves, 1948 National League Pennant Winners." This aerial photograph shows the huge scoreboard that was installed in left field prior to the beginning of the 1949 season.

Publisher: Colourpicture Publications, Boston, MA, Card No. B53,K2253 * Manufacturer: Colourpicture Publications * Type: Linen * Postmark: Boston, MA, June 7, 1949 * Value Index: D

Vern "Junior" Stephens was one of the hardest hitting short-stops in Baseball, leading the American League in HRs in one season and RBIs in three seasons. The 5-foot-6-inch, 185-pound righthanded hitter liked the short left field wall at Boston's Fenway Park. In 1949 he had a career high of 39 HRs, and a League-leading 159 RBI. Stephens began his Major League playing in 1941 with the St. Louis Browns and was traded to the Boston Red Sox in 1948. His 15 years in Baseball ended in 1955 with the Chicago White Sox, with an overall .286 BA.

Publisher: J.D. (Charlie) McCarthy, Royal Oak, MI * Manufacturer: Not Indicated * Type: Black & White * Postmark: Not Used * Value Index: C

In 1947, owner Tom Yawkee of the Red Sox decided to install lights at Fenway Park. This photograph shows the lights shining on the playing field. Yawkee had been against the use of lights until he noted that almost every other team was playing night Baseball. The Red Sox had won the 1946 Pennant and had 1,416,944 fans (the first time their attendance had exceeded 1,000,000 fans). In 1947 the team finished in third place, yet they had more fans in attendance. This increase can be attributed to the installation of the lights for night games.

Fenway Park—Home of the Boston Red Sox, Boston, Mass.

Publisher: Tichnor Bros., Inc., Boston, MA, Card No. 51,78552 * Manufacturer: Tichnor Bros., Inc. * Type: Linen * Postmark: Boston, MA, May 7, 1949 * Value Index: D

This aerial view of Fenway Park provides an excellent perspective of the park in the late 1940s. Lights had been installed in 1947 and the seating was for approximately 35,000 fans. The seats were arranged to be close to the action and the park was an excellent place to watch a game. There is a clear view of the left field wall popularly known as the "Green Monster." All advertisements had been removed from the wall in 1947 and it was painted green. The dimensions of the park had been changed at different times until 1947 and they have remained unchanged to date. The distances are 315 feet along the left field foul line, with 389 feet to center field, and 302 feet along the right field foul line.

Fenway Park, Boston, Massachusetts   B54

Publisher: Colourpicture Publications, Boston, MA, Card No. B54, K2254 * Colourpictures Publications * Type: Linen * Postmark: Boston, MA, July 5, 1950 * Value Index: D

There is always a sense of excitement among collectors when a previously unknown item is discovered. Many collectors of Baseball Picture Postcards are pleased to find the Advertising Postcards that apply to their collections. These Postcards are issued by businesses operated by current or former Major League Players, including restaurants, automobile dealerships, etc., and clearly show a ball park and/or players in the background. This Postcard was located by Mike Walsh, Levittown, Pennsylvania who had a sense of exhilaration when he discovered it as issued by Noyes Buick in Boston. It shows an artist's rendering of Braves Field located between the Noyes Buick showroom and the parts and service buildings. This Postcard was sent to a potential customer a few months after the Boston Braves won the National League Pennant in 1948.

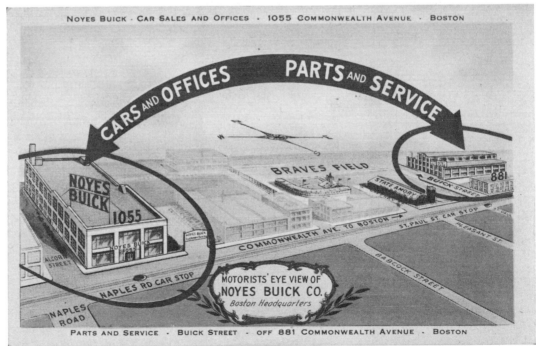

NOYES BUICK · CAR SALES AND OFFICES · 1055 COMMONWEALTH AVENUE · BOSTON

CARS AND OFFICES   PARTS AND SERVICE

BRAVES FIELD

MOTORISTS' EYE VIEW OF NOYES BUICK CO. Boston Headquarters

PARTS AND SERVICE · BUICK STREET · OFF 881 COMMONWEALTH AVENUE · BOSTON

Publisher: Colourpicture Publications, Boston, MA, Card No. 17,547 * Manufacturer: Colourpicture Publications * Type: Linen * Postmark: Boston, MA, December 29, 1948 * Value Index A

In 1950 the Philadelphia Phillies won their first Pennant since 1915 largely as a result of righthanded pitcher Robin Roberts. He was 22 years old when he signed a contract to play Baseball after his graduation from Michigan State University in 1948. During the 1948 season with the Phillies he won 7 and lost 9 games with a 3.15 ERA. In 1949 he won 15 and lost 15 games, and in 1950 he established himself as a star player with 20 wins and 11 losses.

The year 1950 began a series of six consecutive seasons in which he won at least 20 games; 28 wins in 1952 and a League-leading 23 wins in 1953, 1954, and 1955. Roberts had a high-velocity fast ball with exceptional control. During his 19 years in Baseball he walked 902 batters and had 2,357 strike outs. Considering that he pitched more than 200 innings per season his average was slightly more than one walk per game. He was elected into the Hall of Fame after his career ended.

Publisher: Not Indicated * Manufacturer: Not Indicated * Type: Real Photograph * Postmark: Not Used * Value Index: B

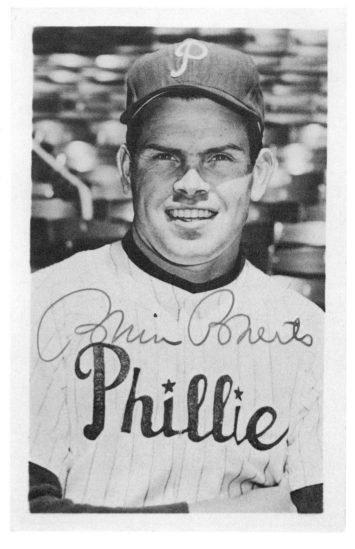

Curt Simmons was almost the equal of Robin Roberts on the pitching mound during the 1950 Pennant-winning season. When the two young pitchers signed their bonus contracts in 1947 Simmons received $65,000 and Roberts received $25,000. When Ty Cobb saw Simmons win a high school Babe Ruth All Star Game at the Polo Grounds, he was so impressed with Simmons' batting skills that he suggested to Curt that he should concentrate on hitting and play the outfield rather than pitching. Simmons drove in the winning run while playing the outfield and he also pitched during the game. Curt decided to remain a pitcher and did so without any regrets. He won 17 and lost 8 games without participating in the World Series against the Yankees because he was called into military service one month before the season ended. We can presume that he would have been a 20-game winner if he had not entered service. This Postcard was produced by the Pennsylvania Dairy Council and has a message from Simmons to drink milk and enjoy good health. The clean-living Simmons, from nearby Egypt, Pennsylvania, was a fine spokesman for the Dairy Council.

Publisher: Dairy Council * Manufacturer: Not Indicated * Type: Black & White * Postmark: Not Used * Value Index: B

When the Philadelphia Phillies won the 1950 Pennant the major portion of their offense was provided by rightfielder Del Ennis who had a League-leading 126 RBI. He was able to respond to the pressure of a tight Pennant race by providing the important hits and the ability to drive in the winning runs. His .311 BA was the second best of his career and his 31 HRs was the fifth best in the National League. The HR record is more impressive when you consider that he played in Connie Mack Stadium, always a difficult stadium to hit home runs. Ennis had the misfortune to be with teams that seldom won a Pennant. The year 1950 was an exception and he was ready to perform as he did to move his team forward.

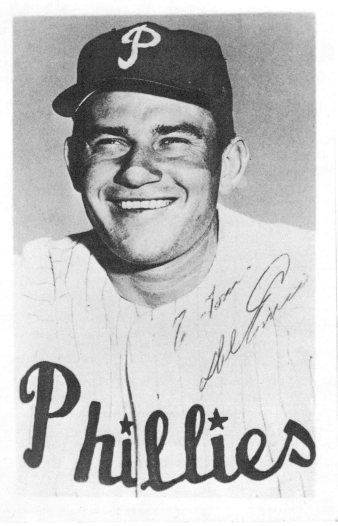

Publisher: J.J.K. Copy-Art, New York, NY * Manufacturer: J.J.K. Copy-Art * Type: Real Photograph * Postmark: Jenkintown, PA, September 19, 1955 * Value Index: B

This aerial photograph of Yankee Stadium shows the mammoth stadium in the 1950s and the World Series decorations that it had for many of those years. The decorations were hung out for every year except 1954 when Cleveland won the Pennant, and 1959, when the Chicago White Sox won the Pennant.

Publisher: Not Indicated * Manufacturer: Not Indicated *Type: Chrome * Postmark: Not Used * Value Index: C

Shortstop Phil Rizzuto played for 13 years with the New York Yankees and is a example of how a person small in stature can become an outstanding Major League star. Although he was only 5 feet-6 inches tall and weighed less than 150 pounds, Rizzuto was a prime reason why the Yankees won nine American League Pennants and won the World Series in seven of the nine years. Years after Phil became one of the best players in Baseball, Yankee General Manager Ed Barrow joked about how Phil became a Yankee. "We signed him for 15 cents, a 10-cent phone call to his home in Glendale, Long Island and a nickel for the cup of coffee we gave him when he showed up at the stadium." Rizzuto was turned down by the Brooklyn

Publisher: Louis Dormand, Riverhead, Long Island, NY * Manufacturer: Not Indicated * Type: Chrome * Postmark: Not Used * Value Index: C

Dodgers and the New York Giants as being too small when he applied as a 5-foot, 17-year-old player from Richmond Hills High School. He did not impress either team management. He was given the nickname "Scooter" because of his small size and his ability to move around the bases. His speed and fielding ability were obvious; however, his batting surprised everyone. He had a .307 BA when he joined the Yankees in 1941 and helped beat the Dodgers in the World Series four games to one. In 1950 Phil had an outstanding season with a .324 BA and won the League Most Valuable Player Award. This photograph was taken in 1954, near the end of his career. When he retired after the 1956 season, Rizzuto became a Yankee broadcaster and he remains as one of the team's play-by-play announcers.

This photograph is on the only known commercially produced Postcard of Griffith Stadium and shows a capacity crowd for opening day for of the 1951 Season. Unfortunately, the Washington Senators generally faded into the oblivion of the second division by June or July of each year. "First In War, First In Peace and Last in the American League" was a prophetic expression for the fans. Two pleasant exceptions to this rule were in 1924 and 1925 when Bucky Harris led them to two American League Pennants and the 1924 World Series Championship. Pitcher Walter Johnson won the seventh and deciding game (at the age of 37 and near the end of his fabulous career) against the New York

GRIFFITH STADIUM OPENING DAY

Publisher: Eastern Air Advertising Service, Washington, DC * Manufacturer: Not Indicated * Type: Black & White * Postmark: New York, NY April 22, 1954 * Value Index: A

Giants. A tradition was begun on opening day in 1910 when President William Howard Taft threw out the first baseball to mark the beginning of a new season.

Although the umpire is disliked by the players and the fans, he is an important part of every game. The umpire calls the balls and strikes, decides when a player is safe or out, and interprets the rules of the game. It is a thankless job, where someone thinks the umpire is incorrect at least 50 percent of the time. Umpires work as hard as the players to keep the game running smoothly and receive much less salary than the players. For many years American League umpire Bill McGowan was considered one of the best in the Major Leagues. He realized the importance of training young men to became umpires. This rare illustration shows instructor Augie Donatelli, a highly respected National League umpire, explaining the details of making a

DONATELLI INSTRUCTING

BILL McGOWAN'S SCHOOL for UMPIRES
DATONA BEACH, FLORIDA—1952

Publisher: Grogan Photo Co., Danville, IL * Manufacturer: Grogan Photo Co. * Type: Real Photograph * Postmark: Not Used * Value Index: A

call on the bases. While it is important to learn the rudiments of the game from an umpire's viewpoint he must also be able to respond properly to the pressures of the game. A story is told about Bill McGowan. Baseball historian Lee Allen said in the opening game of the 1939 World Series, Cincinnati Pitcher Paul Derringer lost the game against Red Ruffing of the Yankees based on a 2 to 1 score. Derringer, known to have a strong temper, asked to see McGowan who was the umpire behind home plate. McGowan expected to feel the wrath of Derringer who was upset at losing the game. Instead Derringer said, "Bill, I just want to tell you that's the greatest job of calling balls and strikes I've ever seen. You didn't miss a call all afternoon." This comment was an important indication of respect for one of the best umpires in Baseball history. Bill McGowan enter the Hall of Fame in August 1992.

Ernie Harwell (who wrote the Introduction to this book) is the only Major League broadcaster to be traded for a Baseball player. The long time "Voice of the Detroit Tigers" and member of the Baseball Hall of Fame developed an outstanding reputation as a broadcaster for Earl Mann's Atlanta Crackers of the Southern Association. He was considered an outstanding broadcaster to the extent that he attracted the attention of Brooklyn General Manager Branch Rickey, who wanted to hire him as the Dodger announcer. Mann did not wish to stand in Harwell's way; however, he considered himself to be in a good bargaining position and he was always looking for good players. Mann requested that Rickey send catcher Cliff Daper

Publisher: Not Indicated * Manufacturer: Not Indicated * Type: Real Photograph * Postmark: Not Used * Value Index: A

to him for the release of Harwell from his contract. After broadcasting Dodger games for a few years he was hired by the New York Giants at a higher salary. This photograph shows Harwell broadcasting for radio station WMCA at the Polo Grounds during a Giants game in the early 1950s. One of the subtle nuances of this illustration shows two packages of Chesterfield cigarettes prominently displayed near the microphone. Ernie has always been a nonsmoker; however, Chesterfields was the sponsor of the broadcasts. In 1954, Ernie became the first announcer for the Baltimore Orioles and in 1960 he went to Detroit as the Tiger announcer until the end of the 1991 season. In 1992, he began broadcasting the CBS Radio "Game of the Week."

If a free-swinging slugger is your favorite type of Baseball player, you would have enjoyed watching Gus Zernial. Gus swung from the heels on almost every pitch, and when he connected, good things usually happened. He was handsome and 25 years old when he joined the Chicago White Sox in 1949. He had a broken collarbone and played only one-half of the season. In 1950 he had recovered from his injury, hitting 29 HRs and 93 RBI. He also led the American League with 110 strike-outs. Only four games into the 1951 season he was traded to the Philadelphia Athletics, where he led the League with 33 HRs and 124 RBI. In his typical feast-or-famine approach he also led the League with 101 strike-outs. In 1953 he had 42 HRs and 108 RBI. In 1954 a second broken collarbone reduced him to 14 HRs. In 1955, with the Athletics playing in Kansas City, he had 30 HRs second to League-leader Mickey Mantle who had 37 HRs. Zernial's career ended in 1959 with the Detroit Tigers where he played on a limited basis as a first baseman. During 11 Major League seasons Gus had 237 HRs, 776 RBI, 755 strike-outs, and a .256 BA.

Publisher: Olmes Studio, Philadelphia, PA * Manufacturer: Olmes Studio * Type: Real Photograph * Postmark: Philadelphia, PA, August 30, 1952 * Value Index: A

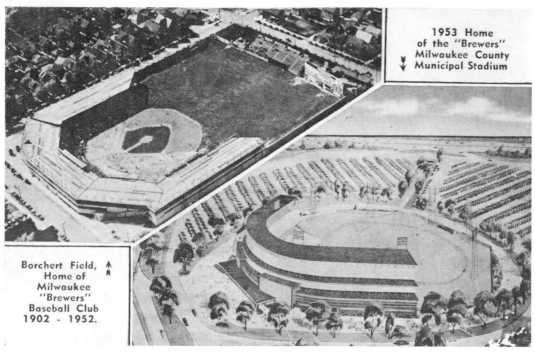

1953 Home of the "Brewers" Milwaukee County Municipal Stadium

Borchert Field, Home of Milwaukee "Brewers" Baseball Club 1902 - 1952.

Publisher: E.C. Kropp company, Milwaukee, WI, Card No. 4953N * Manufacturer: E.C. Dropp Company * Type: black & White * Postmark: Not Used * Value Index: A

When Milwaukee's $5,000,000 County Stadium was nearing completion in 1953 it was scheduled to become the home of the Milwaukee Brewers of the American Association. The Brewers were the top Minor League farm club of the Boston Braves who owned the Brewer franchise. The Braves had lost more than $1,000,000 during the previous three seasons in Boston because of dwindling attendance at Braves Field. The completion of County Stadium brought an immediate response from the Perini brothers who owned the Braves and the Brewers. On March 18, 1953, while the Braves were in spring training at Bradenton, the Perini brothers announced the immediate move of the Braves to Milwaukee. This dual illustration, including an artist's sketch, is the first view of the County Stadium. It also shows Borchert Field, home to the Minor League Brewers for more than 50 years.

This photograph shows how Milwaukee County Stadium looked on opening day, April 14, 1953 when 53,357 fans filled every available seat and watched the Braves defeat the St. Louis Cardinals in 10 innings by a 3 to 2 score. By the end of this inaugural season at County Stadium, the Braves had a National League record of 1,826,397 fans. This number was a remarkable feat for a new franchise and proved that the Perini Brothers made a sound business decision in moving out of Boston where they had only 281,278 fans in the prior year. When this photograph was taken in 1953 there were only 27,982 permanent seats. Note the additional 7500 temporary bleacher seats along the left-field foul line and in left-center field.

Publisher: L.L. Cook Company, Milwaukee, WI, Card No.16539 * Manufacturer: E.C. Kropp Company, Milwaukee, WI * Type: Linen * Postmark: Not Used * Value Index: D

This photograph also shows the County Stadium in Milwaukee. As in the previous scene this photograph was taken during the first season in 1953. Although the Braves slipped from a second place finish in 1953 to third place in 1954 attendance was better in 1954. During the off-season approximately 9,000 seats were added, bringing the total capacity to over 43,000. The fans came to the games in record numbers with 2,131,388 people passing through the turnstiles during that year.

Publisher: Barg & Foster Candy Company, Milwaukee, WI * Manufacturer: Dexter Press, West Nyack, NY * Type: Chrome * Postmark: Milwaukee, WI, March 1954 * Value Index: D

This aerial photograph of the Milwaukee County Stadium shows the results of the expansion between the 1953 and 1954 seasons. There are permanent bleachers in the right field and center field areas. The information on the back of the Postcard explains that this photograph was taken on the day the Braves became the first National League team to have more than 2,000,000 fans in one season. This was a portent of events to come, as the Braves had more than 2,000,000 fans during each of the next four years, ending with a League Pennant and a World Series victory over the Yankees in 1957. During that time period the City of Milwaukee was the Baseball Capital of the world and County Stadium had become Baseball's shrine.

Publisher: L.L. Cook Company, Milwaukee, WI * Manufacturer: Curt Teich Company, Chicago, IL * Type: Linen * Postmark: Milwaukee, WI, April 21, 1957 * Value Index: D

Curt Gowdy is one of the best-known Major League broadcasters. He began as assistant to Mel Allen during the New York Yankee broadcasts in 1949. His career blossomed when he became the Boston Red Sox No. 1 broadcaster and the play-by-play Voice of Baseball on NBC TV. In his autobiography, COWBOY AT THE MIKE, Gowdy credits his Yankee partner Mel Allen with much of his success. "Allen was the hardest working broadcaster I ever knew. At the time I joined him in New York, he was the hottest sports announcer in the business, but he never let down, never eased off, never missed a detail. He made me pay close attention to everything that happened, not only on the field but in the stands. He had the great faculty of picking up the sidelights that help give the listener the feel of the ballpark." After college, Gowdy worked for radio station KFBC in Cheyenne, WY, before he moved to KOMA in Oklahoma City and began broadcasting Baseball games for the Oklahoma City Indians of the Texas League. This Minor League experience provided the background for his selection to work with Allen. This photograph, taken at Cleveland's Municipal Stadium, shows the "Voice of the Red Sox" in 1951. Note the oversize microphone in use at that time, compared to the pencil-sized microphones used today.

Publisher: Fine Arts Studio, Cleveland, OH, Card No. 64991 * Manufacturer: Dexter Press Inc., West Nyack, NY * Type: Chrome * Postmark: Not Used * Value Index: A

An examination of the success of the New York Yankees during the 1950s and 1960s, indicates that much of the credit must go to lefthanded pitcher Whitey Ford. During his 16 seasons in the Major Leagues, he was on 11 Pennant-and 7 World Series-winning Yankee teams. At the end of his career in 1967, Ford had won 236 and lost only 106 games, for a .690 winning percentage. This percentage was the second best in the history of Baseball. Whitey was so reliable that he won almost 7 of every 10 games. At 5 feet-10 inches tall, and 178 pounds, he was not an overpowering pitcher. He had superb control, excellent breaking pitches, and a fine changeup pitch. He kept the batters off balance by changing speeds and placing the ball exactly where he wanted it to go. In his rookie season, 1950, he endeared himself to Yankee fans by winning nine games and losing one, while winning one game in the World Series against the Philadelphia Phillies. After he returned from military service, he won 18 and lost 6 games. In 1955 he was the American League's top pitcher with 18 wins and 7 losses, and won two games in the World Series. He was the top pitcher in 1961 with 25 wins and 4 losses and in 1963 with 24 wins and 7 losses. In the World Series he won and lost more games than any other pitcher—10 wins and 8 losses. Ford was the ultimate finesse pitcher and his nicknames "Slick" and "Chairman of the Board" indicated his high regard.

Publisher: Louis Dormand, Riverhead, NY, Card No. 1913 * Manufacturer: Not Indicated * Type: Chrome * Postmark: Not Used * Value Index: C

Publisher: Louis Dormand, Riverhead, NY, Card No. 65429 * Manufacturer: Not Indicated * Type: Chrome * Postmark: Not Used * Value Index: C

This photograph of New York Yankee first baseman Johnny Mize was taken in 1953, at the age of 40, and in his final Baseball season. He was almost exclusively a pinch hitter with the Yankees in 1953 and had a .250 BA. He had 6 HRs and 27 RBI, making a significant contribution to another Pennant for the "Bronx Bombers." During his earlier years with the St. Louis Cardinals his graceful actions in the field gave him the nickname "The Big Cat" despite his 6-foot-2-inch, 215-pound size. In 1939, with the Cardinals, he won the National League Batting Championship; he had a .349 BA. Two years earlier he posted a .364 BA, but finished second to teammate Joe Medwick's .374 BA. Before joining the Yankees in 1949, Mize won the National League HR title four times and RBI title three times. He ended his career in the top three hitting categories 54 times and had a final career .312 BA. Mize was elected to the Baseball Hall of Fame in 1981.

Allie Reynolds was called "Superchief" because he was part Cherokee Indian and possessed one of the best fastballs in the American League. Reynolds had 13 successful seasons in the Major Leagues. Ironically, his career began with the Cleveland Indians. He joined the "Tribe" in late 1942 and pitched only two innings. He remained with Cleveland through 1946 winning 51 and losing 47 games. He was traded to the New York Yankees before the beginning of the 1947 season and had 19 wins and 8 losses. He was an important factor in the winning of the Pennant and World Series for that year. He won the second World Series game by a 10 to 3 score. Reynolds won 16 games in 1948, 17 in 1949, 16 in 1950, 17 in 1951, 20 in 1952, 13 in 1953, and 13 in 1954. During that time he also had 7 wins and 2 losses in the various World Series. During his 8 years in New York he won 131 and lost 58 games. This photograph shows him warming up at Yankee Stadium.

Publisher: Louis Dormand, Riverhead, NY, Card No. 65429 * Manufacturer: Not Indicated * Type: Chrome * Postmark: Not Used * Value Index: C

Ed Lopat was an almost exact opposite of Allie Reynolds. Despite their differences, they complimented each other very well as outstanding Yankee pitchers. Lopat was a lefthander in contrast to Reynolds, a righthander. Reynolds relied on a blazing fastball and Lopat was known as a "junk ball" pitcher with three speeds—slow, slower, and slowest. Lopat came to the Yankees in 1948 from the Chicago White Sox where he had 50 wins in four seasons with a weak-hitting team. His record had a dramatic change when he joined the Yankees because they had the dominant hitters in Baseball, led by the future Hall-of-Famer Joe DiMaggio. Lopat won 17 games in 1948, 15 in 1949, 18 in 1950, 21 in 1951, 10 in 1952, 16 in 1953, and 12 in 1954. He lost only 48 games in these years.

Overall, for his 12 years in the Major Leagues he had 166 wins and 112 losses. A safe assumption is that, if Ed Lopat and Allie Reynolds had not played together, the Yankee teams of the late 1940s and early 1950s would not have been as outstanding as they were.

Publisher: Louis Dormand, Riverhead, NY, Card No. 65423 * Manufacturer: Not Indicated * Type: Chrome * Postmark: Not Used * Value Index: C

Righthander Johnny Sain was a pitcher who had three highly successful careers in the Major Leagues. As a starting pitcher with the Boston Braves in the late 1940s, he won 20 games in 1946, 21 games in 1947, and 24 games in 1948, when he pitched the Braves to a National League Pennant. He missed three seasons in 1943, 1944, and 1945 because of military service. During that time we can assume that Sain would have added 50 to 70 victories to his 139 career wins. He had an exceptional curve ball, a fine fastball, excellent control, and was considered one of the most clever pitchers of the time. His second successful career began with the New York Yankees when he became one of the top relief pitchers during the 1952, 1953, and 1954 seasons. Although the Yankees finished second to Cleveland during the 1954 season, Sain led the League with 22 games saved. Sain retired at the end of the 1955 season and later became recognized as one of the finest pitching coaches with several Major League teams. Although he is not a member of the Hall of Fame he merits close scrutiny when one considers his outstanding careers in Baseball.

Publisher: Louis Dormand, Riverhead, NY, Card No. 1912 * Manufacturer: Not Indicated * Type: Chrome * Postmark: Not Used * Value Index: C

During the time when the Canadians did not have their own major league teams, many Canadian Baseball fans would depend on the nearby American games. They would cross the border at Windsor, Ontario to watch the games at Detroit. Although Cleveland was a little farther away for Canadian fans they were within easy flying time by Trans Canada Airlines. This illustration is an advertising Postcard which promotes the ease of flying from Toronto to Cleveland. It was produced in 1953 in time for the 1954 Baseball season. The scene emphasizes the idea by showing an airplane flying over Municipal Stadium, home of the Cleveland Indians.

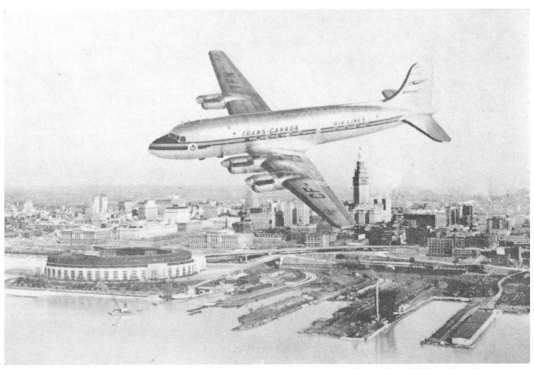

Publisher: Trans Canada Airlines, Toronto, Canada * Manufacturer: Not Indicated * Type: Black & White * Postmark: Not Used * Value Index A

April 15, 1954 was a very important day in the history of Baltimore. After losing an American League franchise to New York in 1902, Baltimore finally had a major league team. A crowd of 46,354 eager fans, as shown in this photograph, came to see the Orioles win over the Chicago White Sox by a 3 to 1 score.

Unfortunately, the Orioles quickly sank into oblivion, ending the season with 54 wins and 100 losses for the worst record in the American League. If there was any solace for the Oriole fans the Pittsburgh Pirates in the National League ended the season with 53 wins and 101 losses. During that initial 1954 season, despite the poor showing, the Orioles had a remarkable attendance record of 1,060,910 fans. During the prior year when the franchise was in St.

Publisher: Baltimore Orioles, Baltimore, MD * Manufacturer: Not Indicated * Type: Real Photograph * Postmark: Not Used * Value Index: A

Louis as the Browns the attendance was only 297,238. Bill Veeck, beleaguered by cash-flow problems and debt, reluctantly sold the franchise to a group of Baltimore businessmen headed by Clarence W. Miles and James Keelty, Jr.

If the 1954 Orioles had a bright spot it was flame-throwing righthanded pitcher Bob Turley. He was called "Bullet Bob" because of his blinding pitching speed. Turley pitched the entire opening day game against the White Sox winning by a 3 to 1 score, scattering seven hits, and striking out nine batters before the wildly enthusiastic crowd. Turley gave the Baltimore fans 14 wins and 15 losses during that first season. Many of the losses were classified as "heartbreakers" as, for example, the first night game in Memorial Stadium played against the Cleveland Indians. Turley was pitching a no hitter with one man out in the ninth inning and leading by a 1 to 0 score. He lost the game by a 2 to 1 score on a double by Al Rosen and a HR by Larry Doby. He lost many well-pitched games because his teammates failed to produce many runs. This photograph was taken in Yuma, Arizona during the Oriole's first spring training and shows Bullet Bob following through on his pitching delivery. After the first season with the Orioles, Turley went to the New York Yankees as part of a 17-player trade. He had success in New York, leading American League pitchers by winning 21 games in 1958.

Publisher: Baltimore Orioles, Baltimore, MD * Manufacturer: Not Indicated * Type: Real Photograph * Postmark: Not Used * Value Index: B

Perhaps the rarest chrome-type stadium Picture Postcard produced in the 1950s is this exterior front view of Baltimore's Memorial Stadium. Although a beautiful view the production of this Postcard was apparently very limited. The stadium was built at a cost of $6,000,000, was financed by two bond issues, and construction began in 1949. The stadium was double-decked, built on 28-3/4 acres of city land, and completed in the Fall-Winter of 1953-1954. During that time the St. Louis Browns were sold to Baltimore investors and the team was moved to Baltimore. The stadium was dedicated to the veterans who fought in our various wars. Memorial Stadium has a proud tradition as the Orioles have won six American League Pennants and three World Series since opening in 1954. The stadium has been replaced by a new stadium in Baltimore's Inner Harbor area in 1992.

Publisher: Levi-Shall Inc., Card No. SI6160 * Manufacturer: Not Indicated * Type: Chrome * Postmark: Not Used * Value Index: A

When people think of Hank Aaron, the first impression is that he is the man who broke Babe Ruth's career HR record to become the all-time HR king. Hank Aaron was actually an excellent all-around player, with a lifetime .305 BA, and outstanding defensive outfielder with a fine throwing arm. He was teamed with his brother Tommie, to become one of only a few brother combinations in major league Baseball. This photograph was taken in 1963 at the Milwaukee County Stadium when Tommie joined the Braves. Tommie's career lasted only four mediocre seasons during which he had a .229 BA while Hank was the dominant National League hitter during the 1950s. He joined Milwaukee in 1954 from the Negro National League and showed his potential with a .280

Publisher: H.F. Gardner, Chicago, IL, Card No. C15066 * Manufacturer: Not Indicated * Type: Chrome * Postmark: Not Used * Value Index: B

BA during that first season hitting 13 HRs and 69 RBI. In 1955 he had a 314 BA, 27 HRs and 106 RBI. His success continued with improvements every year and in 1959 he won his second National League batting championship with a .355 BA, 39 HRs, and 123 RBI. His fabulous career ended in 1976 and he left a target of 755 HRs for future sluggers.

Harold "Pee Wee" Reese earned his nickname by winning a marble tournament when he was 12 years old. His fame was acquired as a shortstop and captain of the Brooklyn Dodgers. Reese played 16 seasons with the Dodgers beginning in 1940. He missed the seasons of 1943, 1944, and 1945 while in the U.S. Navy during World War II. He was an extremely fine shortstop performing well in all aspects of the game. He had excellent range in the infield, a fine throwing arm, high speed on the bases, and hit the ball with surprising power. He played next to second baseman Jackie Robinson for ten years. Although there is much said about Robinson's ability to steal bases, Reese had more stolen bases in 6 of these 10 years. During Pee Wee's 16 seasons, the Dodgers won 7 Pennants and a World Series in 1955 by four games to three over the New York Yankees. Reese was consistent, with a career .269 BA and a .272 BA for the 7 World Series in which he played. This photograph was taken in 1954 when he attained his season-highest .309 BA. His value to the Dodgers was in the fact that, as team captain, he was admired by the players and the management.

Publisher: Louis Dormand, Riverhead, NY, Card No. 3591 * Manufacturer: Not Indicated * Type: Chrome * Postmark: Not Used * Value Index: C

The 1954 Cleveland Indians ran roughshod over their American League opponents, winning a record number of 111 games and finishing 8 games in front of the defending World Champion Yankees. The Tribe ended a string of five straight Yankee Pennants and World Series championships. Manager Al Lopez had the team in first place by May 10 as they combined brilliant pitching, fine defense, and power hitting. Third baseman Al Rosen provided much of Cleveland's power with 24 HRs, 102 RBI, and a .300 BA. He was Most Valuable Player in 1953 and almost earned the title in 1954; however, it was given to Yankee catcher Yogi Berra. Although he joined the Indians in 1947 he did not become the regular third basemen until 1950 with 37 HRs and 116 RBI. His career was brief, as he retired in 1956; however, he will be remembered by Cleveland fans as one of the best players in Indian history.

Publisher: Cleveland Indians, Cleveland, OH * Manufacturer: Not Indicated * Type: Real Photograph * Postmark: Miami Beach, FL, January 5, 1953 * Value Index: C

Mike Garcia of the Cleveland Indians was known as the "Big Bear" and he played a key role in the success of the Indians, winning the Pennant in 1954. The burley righthander Garcia with pitchers Bob Lemon and Early Wynn, formed "The Big Three," recognized as the finest pitching staff in Baseball. Garcia led the American League with a 2.64 ERA while winning 19 and losing only 8 games. Lemon and Wynn each won 23 games during the 1954 season, had a slightly higher ERA than Garcia, and held the opposing teams to less than 3 runs per game. Cleveland was the favorite to win the World Series. The underdog National League Champion New York Giants upset the Indians in four straight games. Garcia was the starter and loser in game No. 3 by a 6 to 2 score. This photograph of Mike Garcia shows the 200-pound Big Bear putting all of his weight behind a fast ball. Garcia won 20 games in 1951, 22 in 1952, and had a career total of 142 wins and 92 losses with a 3.27 ERA.

Mike Garcia

Publisher: Cleveland Indians, Cleveland, OH * Manufacturer: Not Indicated * Type: Real Photograph * Postmark: Cleveland, OH, August 16, 1952 * Value Index: C

Bob Lemon

Hall-of-Fame righthand pitcher Bob Lemon has the distinction of pitching in the only two World Series in which Cleveland appeared during the last 70 years. In 1920 the Indians won the American League Pennant and won the World Series over the Brooklyn Dodgers. In 1948 the Tribe made its second appearance in a World Series and won the title, defeating Boston four games to two. Lemon joined the Indians in 1946 and became a star with 20 wins and 14 losses in 1948. Lemon won 2 games without a loss in the 1948 World Series but lost 2 games in 1954 against the Giants. During his 13 years with the Indians he had seven 20-victory seasons. His success as a pitcher is remarkable considering that he began as an infielder and was converted to pitcher at the age of 26 by manager Lou Boudreau.

Publisher: Cleveland Indians, Cleveland, OH * Manufacturer: Not Indicated * Type: Real Photograph * Postmark: Cleveland, OH, August 16, 1952 * Value Index: C

Players teased righthand pitcher Early Wynn that if his mother was crowding home plate too much he would hit her with a pitch. "No," Wynn replied, "but I'd brush her back." Wynn was an excellent competitor and earned his place in the Hall of Fame by winning 300 games. He also had the distinction of playing Major League Baseball in four decades, from the 1930s through the 1960s. Early began with the Washington Senators in 1939, but his record of no wins and two losses caused him to be sent back to the Minor League in 1940. He won 18 games for the Senators in 1943 and 17 games with Washington in 1947. Wynn won 20 games for the first time after he was traded to Cleveland, followed by 23 wins in 1952 and 1954. Those 23 wins in 1954 tied him with teammate Bob Lemon for the most victories among American League pitchers. Early was traded to the Chicago White Sox in 1958 and was the outstanding pitcher in the American League in 1959 with 22 wins. The White Sox won their first Pennant in 1959 since 1919. In 1963 Wynn went back to Cleveland where he won his 300th game and then retired that same year.

Publisher: Cleveland Indians, Cleveland, OH * Manufacturer: Not Indicated * Type: Real Photograph * Postmark: Not Used * Value Index: C

Lawrence Peter "Yogi" Berra was unquestionably one of the finest catchers in Baseball history. His 19-year career began at the end of the 1946 season and continued until 1965 when he played in four games with the New York Mets as a player-coach. Except for those four games the remainder of his career was played with the New York Yankees. Berra appeared in a record 14 World Series. With a career .285 BA and 358 HRs he was inducted into the Hall of Fame in 1972. Yogi grew up in the Hill District of St. Louis, living across the street from Joe Garagiola who became a major league catcher and famous sportscaster. Berra acquired his nickname from a boyhood friend, Jack McGuire. McGuire after seeing a motion picture featuring a Hindu fakir (a disciple of Yoga) who was sitting motionless with arms and legs folded and a strong facial expression, said he looked like his pal Berra. From that time on Berra was known as Yogi. Much of the success the Yankees had during Yogi's 18 seasons is directly attributable to Berra who was named the League's Most Valuable Player in 1951, 1954, and 1955. The Yankees lost only 4 of the 14 World Series in which he appeared. A cartoon of Berra's face actually became the inspiration for the Yogi Bear character used in cartoons.

Publisher: Louis Dormand, Riverhead, NY, Card No. 65422 * Manufacturer: Not Indicated * Type: Chrome * Postmark: Not Used * Value Index: B

When the Athletics abandoned Philadelphia for greener pastures in Kansas City they sold the Connie Mack Stadium to the Philadelphia Phillies for an estimated $2,000,000. The historic ball park, originally called Shibe Park (named for the team's first owner) was an all steel and concrete structure. The purchase by the Phillies enabled them to own the ball park they had shared with the Athletics since 1938 when they abandoned the deteriorating Baker Bowl. Although the Athletics had great success in the early years at Shibe Park they had not won a Pennant since 1931, and usually finished near to the bottom of the American League. The Phillies had won a National League Pennant in 1950 with a young team known as the "Whiz Kids." Philadelphia fans, long

Publisher: Art Color Card Distributors, Camden, NJ, Card No. PHI-105,C6918 * Manufacturer: Mike Roberts, Berkeley, CA * Type: Chrome * Postmark: Not Used * Value Index: C

accustomed to losing teams embraced the Phillies and abandoned the Athletics. In 1954, final home attendance for the Athletics was 304,666 compared to 738,991 for the Phillies. In 1953 Shibe Park was renamed Connie Mack Stadium as a tribute to the Athletics owner and manager. The Phillies painted the stadium in the team colors of red and blue and in 1956 obtained a scoreboard from Yankee Stadium after the Yankees purchased a new scoreboard. The Phillies used the stadium until the move into Veterans Stadium in 1971.

At the end of the 1954 season, Chicago industrialist Arnold Johnson purchased the Philadelphia Athletics from Connie Mack and moved the team to Kansas City. A precedent for this move occurred when the financially troubled St. Louis Browns franchise was moved to Baltimore. Kansas City proved ready for the team with excellent fan support. Despite a sixth-place finish, with 63 wins and 91 losses, 1,393,054 fans attended the games, compared to 304,666 in their final season in Philadelphia. Johnson also owned the Kansas City Blues in the American Association, a Triple A farm club for the Yankees. Blues Stadium, built in 1923, held approximately 17,000 spectators and a new stadium was required immediately for Major League Baseball. Johnson

Publisher: J.E. Tetrick, Kansas City, MO, Card No. SK8208 * Manufacturer: Colourpicture, Boston, MA * Type: Chrome * Postmark: Not Used * Value Index: C

sold Blues Stadium for $500,000 to Kansas City and work began immediately to rebuild and doubledeck the facility, renamed Municipal Stadium for the opening of the 1955 season. After working all winter it was ready on April 12, 1955 for 32,844 fans to see President Harry S. Truman throw out the first ball. The Athletics won by a 6 to 2 score over the Detroit Tigers. This illustration is an artist's sketch for the first Postcard issued for Municipal Stadium.

Most of the Baseball Advertising Postcards had previously focused on the players. More businesses, particularly hotels, motels and restaurants began to realize the importance of stressing their close proximity to major league ball parks. One of the pioneers was the Colonial Motel in Kansas City, Kansas. This rare illustration shows the many sightseeing opportunities that guests could enjoy in the area. The people were proud of the team as shown by the illustration of crowd-filled Municipal Stadium. In 1954 Art Ditmar, with 12 wins, and Alex Kellner, with 11 wins, were the leading pitchers. Hitting was the real strength with left fielder Gus Zernial leading the Athletics with 30 HRs and 84 RBI. Veteran outfielders Elmer Valo and Enos

Publisher: Colonial Motel, Kansas City, KS * Manufacturer: Not Indicated * Type: Chrome * Postmark: Kansas City, KS, December 8, 1956 * Value Index: A

Slaughter had a .364 BA and .322 BA respectively, playing part-time. First baseman Vic Power had an exceptional year with a .319 BA and was a wizard in defense leading the League in putouts, assists, and double plays.

This dual-view Postcard shows the exterior and interior of the Kansas City Municipal Stadium. The building in the foreground of the top photograph was used as offices by the Athletics and is located beyond the fence in left field. The bottom photograph was taken from the seats along the third base foul line. The workers were able to accomplish a remarkable feat by completing the work on Municipal Stadium in only 22 weeks in temperatures that were below zero degrees F. The wind was so strong at times that the workers tied themselves to the roof with ropes. A surprising aspect of the stadium is that 180 HRs (more than any other American League Park) were hit there despite a distance of 330 feet along the left field foul line, 422 feet to center field, and 354 feet along the right field foul line. A strong wind usually blowing toward left field may account for this phenomenon.

Publisher: Kansas Distributing Company, Junction City, KS, Card No. 22261 * Manufacturer: Not Indicated * Type: Chrome * Postmark: Not Used * Value Index: B

This illustration of third baseman George Kell was issued by the Orioles when he joined the team in 1956 near the end of an outstanding American League career. Kell began in the Major Leagues in 1943 with the Philadelphia Athletics, was traded to the Detroit Tigers during 1946, went to the Boston Red Sox in 1952, then to the Chicago White Sox in 1954, and lastly to the Orioles in 1956. He had success with every team. He won the American League batting championship with a .343 BA at Detroit in 1949. In 1950 he had a .340 BA and 101 RBI. When he joined the Orioles in 1956, manager Paul Richards wanted Kell for his teaching skills and playing ability. A young third baseman, Brooks Robinson, was considered to have an outstanding future. Kell worked tirelessly with him teaching him all the tricks. When George retired after the 1957 season, he knew his protege was ready to take over third base. As proof of their abilities Kell and Robinson were eventually elected to the Hall of Fame.

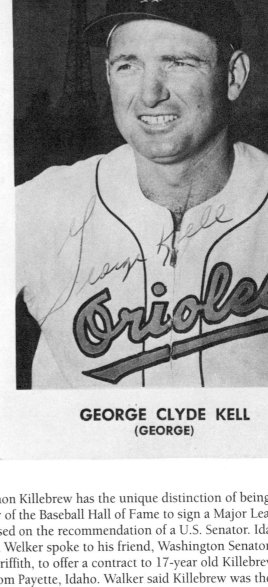

GEORGE CLYDE KELL
(GEORGE)

Publisher: Baltimore Orioles, Baltimore, MD * Manufacturer: Not Indicated * Type: Real Photograph * Postmark: Not Used * Value Index: B

Harmon Killebrew has the unique distinction of being the only member of the Baseball Hall of Fame to sign a Major League contract based on the recommendation of a U.S. Senator. Idaho Senator Herman Welker spoke to his friend, Washington Senator owner Clark Griffith, to offer a contract to 17-year old Killebrew who came from Payette, Idaho. Walker said Killebrew was the best Baseball player that he ever saw and he would become better than Mickey Mantle. Although Killebrew never had Mantle's speed or ability to hit for a higher BA, Harmon did hit more HRs than Mickey. Welker had seen Killebrew hit some prodigious HRs while playing high school and semipro baseball in Payette. Ossie Bluege, the Senators farm director, went to Idaho to see Killebrew and returned impressed. He recommended signing Harmon to a bonus contract of $30,000, the highest ever paid to date by the Senators. Although Killebrew initially struggled at the plate, he showed the potential that enabled him to enjoy a 22-year Major League career with the Senators and Minnesota Twins. His career .256 BA and his 573 HRs ranked fifth on the all-time list. Harmon tied or led the American League six times in HRs and he hit 40 or more HRs on eight occasions. He played third base, outfield, and first base to make Welker's prediction of greatness become a reality. Harmon was 19 years old when this photograph was taken.

Publisher: Don Wingfield, Alexandria, VA * Manufacturer: Not Indicated * Type: Chrome * Postmark: Not Used * Value Index: B

This photograph was taken in 1954 when Enos "Country" Slaughter, a gentleman farmer from North Carolina, was with the New York Yankees and the best years of his career were behind him. He was 38 years old and had been in the Major Leagues since 1938 when he joined the St. Louis Cardinals. Slaughter played Baseball only one way—that was to go "all out". His dash to home plate from first base in the last of the eighth inning gave the Cardinals a 4 to 3 win over the Boston Red Sox in the seventh game of the 1946 World Series. Slaughter was with the Yankees to the end of 1954 and was traded to the Kansas City Athletics early in 1955. Midway through the 1956 season he was traded back to the Yankees and was an important factor in their World Series win over the Dodgers, finishing with a .350 BA and 4 RBIs. In 1959 he retired with a career .300 BA and he later entered the Hall of Fame.

Publisher: Louis Dormand, Riverhead, NY, Card No. 8023 * Manufacturer: Not Indicated * Type: Chrome * Postmark: Not Used * Value Index: B

Mickey Mantle followed another Yankee centerfielder and Hall-of-Famer Joe DiMaggio by opening a restaurant in his hometown of Joplin, Missouri. This photograph was taken inside the Dugout Lounge of Mantle's restaurant at the Holiday Inn of Joplin. Mantle's restaurant did not have the glitter of Fisherman's Wharf in San Francisco, where DiMaggio's restaurant was located. However, it did provide Mickey with background and familiarity in the restaurant business, experience for his current location in New York City. He is no longer associated with the business in Joplin and he now resides in Dallas, Texas and New York City. Despite an arrested case of osteomyelitis, numerous injuries, and frequent surgery on his knees (which bothered him during his entire career) Mantle is remembered as one of the fastest base runners who also hit some of the longest HRs. Mantle hit one HR 565 feet out of Washington's Griffith Stadium. After 18 years, all with the Yankees, Mantle had 536 HRs and a .298 lifetime BA.

Publisher: Holiday Inn, Joplin, MO, Card No. 2DK-33 * Manufacturer: Curt Teich, Chicago, IL * Type: Chrome * Postmark: Not Used * Value Index: B

112

EBBETS FIELD, BROOKLYN, N. Y.   122

Publisher: Foto Seal Company, New York, NY * Manufacturer: Foto Seal Company * Type: Real Photograph * Postmark: Not Used * Value Index: C

The upper photograph, an aerial view of the completely filled Ebbets Field, Brooklyn helps to explain why the Dodgers left Brooklyn for Los Angeles. The ball park was situated on one square block with no room for expansion. Despite the fact the Dodgers won Pennants in 1955 and 1956 the Milwaukee Braves playing in their new County Stadium had almost one million more fans per season. Dodger owner Walter O'Malley realized the Dodgers required larger facilities and hired architect Norman Bel Geddes to see if the 32,000 seating capacity of Ebbets Field could be expanded. The only possibility was to move upward, but adding another deck was not feasible and a new stadium was needed. Initially, a section of land near the Atlantic Avenue Depot of the Long Island Railroad was considered. The city would not, or could not, provide the land. Although O'Malley threatened to move to Los Angeles the City government was convinced the move would not occur. The lower photograph shows Roosevelt Stadium in Jersey City, New Jersey built in 1937 and named after President Franklin D. Roosevelt. It seated 25,000 people with room for 40,000 with standing spectators. The Dodgers played eight additional games at this stadium without good results. After the 1957 season, O'Malley's threat became reality and the Dodgers left. After 1,200,000 fans attended their games in 1957, the Dodgers had an additional 800,000 fans in their first season on the West Coast. A new area had begun.

Publisher: Deluxe Greeting Card Company, Newark, NJ, Card No. 14594 * Manufacturer: Not Indicated * Type: Chrome * Postmark: Not Used * Value Index: A

Righthand pitcher Gene Conley of the Milwaukee Braves had several distinctions. At 6-feet-8-inches tall he was the tallest pitcher to perform in the major leagues, and he was able to play two professional sports at the same time. While he was pitching for the Milwaukee Braves he was also playing basketball with the Boston Celtics of the National Basketball Association. When the Braves won their first Pennant in 1957, Conley won 9 and lost 9 games: 5 wins and 8 losses as a starting pitcher and 4 wins and 1 loss as a relief pitcher. Some people expressed the opinion that if Conley had concentrated on his Baseball, rather than dividing his time between Baseball and basketball, he would have achieved more success than his 11-year career record of 91 wins and 96 losses. This photograph was taken at the Braves spring training camp in Bradenton and provides an indication of the imposing figure he made standing on the pitching mound.

Publisher: Bill & Bob, Bradenton, FL * Manufacturer: Not Indicated * Type: Chrome * Postmark: Milwaukee, WI, November 8, 1956 * Value Index B

When the Braves moved from Boston to Milwaukee in 1953, third baseman Eddie Mathews immediately won the hearts of the Milwaukee fans by hitting 47 HRs to lead the National League. Mathews hit 25 HRs during the Braves final season at Boston; however, the left field fence was 17 feet closer (337 to 320 feet) at County Stadium and Eddie had greater success. At the end of his outstanding career in 1968 he had 512 HRs and was elected to the Hall of Fame. This photograph was taken in Bradenton during Spring training and was released on a promotional Postcard. During Milwaukee's first championship season in 1957 Mathews played a key role hitting 32 HRs, 94 RBI, and had a .292 BA. Mathews and Hank Aaron gave the Braves another Pennant in 1958, but they lost the World Series to the Yankees four games to three.

Publisher: Spic & Span Dry Cleaners, Milwaukee, WI * Manufacturer: Not Indicated * Type: Black & White * Postmark: Not Used * Value Index: C

Warren Spahn won more games than any lefthand pitcher in Baseball history with 363 career wins. Only 4 pitchers, Cy Young, Walter Johnson, Grover Cleveland Alexander, and Christy Mathewson—all righthanders, won more games. Johnny Sain, Spahn's righthanded pitching teammate and one of the best pitching coaches attributed Spahn's success to his intelligence. "Spahn was able to change over from being a power pitcher. He was thorough in his actions. He fielded extremely well, he ran the bases well, and his move to first base was superb. Spahn became great because of these things and because he's one of the smartest men ever to play the game." Spahn, at first base, was able to pick off Jackie Robinson of the Dodgers twice in a crucial game during the 1948 season when Robinson was "King of the Base Stealers." Warren Spahn won 20 or more games 13 times during his 21-year career with the Braves. In 1963, when he was 42 years old, he won 23 and lost 7 games. Spahn's record is remarkable when considering that he did not win his first major league victory until he was 25 years old in 1946. His major league career ended in 1965 after surgery on both knees.

Publisher: Spic & Span Dry Cleaners, Milwaukee, WI * Manufacturer: Not Indicated * Type: Black & White * Postmark: Not Used * Value Index: C

This exterior view of Ebbets Field is an eerie testimony to the bygone days of glory as it shows the front entrance devoid of the crowds that normally gathered. The crowds of fans at the front entrance were shown on the other Postcards issued since 1913 when the park opened. Brooklyn fans continued to support the Dodgers to the end of their stay. In 1957, when the news was out that the Dodgers were leaving more than 1,000,000 fans attended the games at Ebbets Field. From a practical business point of view Walter O'Malley made the correct decision in leaving Brooklyn as the Los Angeles Dodgers became the most successful franchise in Baseball. As far as the loyal Brooklyn Dodger fans are concerned O'Malley is not to be forgiven for taking the team away.

Publisher: Harry H. Baumann, New York, NY, Card No. E-13487 * Manufacturer: Not Indicated * Type: Black & White * Postmark: New York, NY, September 1, 1958 * Value Index: A

Yogi Berra of the Yankees was the dominant catcher in the American League during the 1950s. Roy Campanella of the Dodgers was the best catcher in the National League. Their careers had other similarities. They won Most Valuable Player three times, both were outstanding handlers of their pitchers, and they had an ability to produce timely base hits in important situations. Roy Campanella was born on November 19, 1921 and signed a professional Baseball contract with the Baltimore Elite Giants of the Negro National League when he was 15 years old. He became one of the stars and, after Baseball was integrated in 1947 by Jackie Robinson, Campanella joined the Dodgers in 1948. He had a .258 BA and appeared in 83 games that year. He began a 10-year career, which ended abruptly in the Winter of 1958, when his car skidded on a slick road and crashed against a telephone pole. Roy broke his back and became a paraplegic a few weeks before the beginning of Spring training. Lesser men would have become bitter because of the tragedy but Roy maintained a marvelous attitude. In 1969, when he was inducted into the Hall of Fame, Campanella recalled one of his favorite expressions, "There's a bit of little boy in every good ballplayer." Roy's "little boy attitude" helped him to overcome his problems.

Publisher: Louis Dormand, Riverside, NY, Card No. 3590 * Manufacturer: Not Indicated * Type: Chrome * Postmark: Not Used * Value Index: B

Although Brooklyn's Roy Campanella was considered the best Catcher in the National League, Milwaukee's Del Crandall was considered as No. 2. Crandall became the No. 1 catcher after Campanella's accident. Del was excellent at handling his pitchers, had a fine throwing arm, and had a career .254 BA over 16 Major League Seasons. This photograph was taken during Spring training at Bradenton, FL during the 1950s and shows Del in the on-deck circle waiting for his turn at bat. When the Braves won the first of two consecutive Pennants in 1957 he had a .253 BA and 46 RBI. In 1958 he had a .272 BA and 63 RBI. He was an important part of Milwaukee's success over many years.

Publisher: Bill & Bob, Bradenton, FL, Card No. 13501 * Manufacturer: Not Indicated * Type: Chrome * Postmark: Fullerton, CA * Value Index: B

When the Dodgers left Brooklyn for Los Angeles the New York Giants decided to seek West Coast riches by moving to San Francisco. Owner Horace Stoneham saw attendance dwindling at the Polo Grounds that had been the Giants home since 1891. The neighborhood around the Polo Grounds had been in rapid decline and in the final 1957 season only 653,923 fans attended the games. While the new stadium was being built for the Giants they used Seals Stadium for their home games. Seals Stadium was built in 1931 for $600,000, could hold 18,600, and was considered the best design in minor league parks. The owners, Charles Graham, Jr., Dr. Charles Strub, and George Putnam had spent one year look-

Publisher: Yorkolor Process, New York, NY, Card No. YL7788 * Manufacturer: Not Indicated * Type: Chrome * Postmark: Not Used * Value Index: A

ing at the finest features of other parks and incorporated the best features into Seals Stadium. During their first season the Giants had more than 1,270,000 fans. This photograph was taken along the first base foul line and shows the closeness of the fans to the action on the field. No roof was necessary as the area normally does not have rain and the temperature is very comfortable.

Before Seals Stadium became the home of the San Francisco Giants during 1958 and 1959 the stadium capacity was expanded from 18,600 to 23,000 earlier in 1958. The Giants were in third place in the National League, trailing the Braves by 12 games and the Pirates by 4 games. Despite not being a contender in the Pennant race and playing in the stadium with the smallest seating capacity in the National League, they had more than 1,300,000 fans in 1958 and the same number in 1959, as they again finished in third place. Obviously owner Horace Stoneham was delighted with his move from New York. This photograph of Seals Stadium was taken along the right field foul line and shows the downtown San Francisco skyline only a few blocks away.

Publisher: Yorkolor Process, New York, NY, Card No. YL7789 * Manufacturer: Not Indicated * Type Chrome * Postmark: Not Used * Value Index: A

Willie Mays was one of the most exciting people in Baseball. This multi-talented player was able to do everything required in the game. He had great speed, could hit the ball with power, and was able to reach almost every ball on the fly to center field where he ranked as one of the best defensive outfielders. If he were to be remembered for only one play it would be his catch of a 450-foot drive by Cleveland's Vic Wertz in the first game of the 1954 World Series. The Giants were in a 2 to 2 score, in the 8th inning, with two runners on base. Wertz sent a tremendous drive into deep center field. Mays began running with the crack of the bat and caught the ball over his shoulder while running at full speed in front of the wall at the Polo Grounds. Baseball writer Fred Lieb who had covered World Series games for more than 50 years said it was the greatest catch that he had ever seen. The catch prevented a triple by Wertz and Cleveland did not score the winning run. This play was the climax to an outstanding season where Mays had a .345 BA, hit 41 HRs, and had 110 RBI to easily win the Most Valuable Player award. This photograph shows Mays in a San Francisco uniform shortly after the Giants moved to San Francisco. He was inducted into the Hall of Fame in 1979.

Publisher: J.D. McCarthy, Oak Park, MI * Manufacturer: Not Indicated * Type: Black & White * Postmark: Not Used * Value Index: C

Publisher: Mitock & Sons, Sherman Oaks, CA, Card No. P25137 * Manufacturer: Colourpicture, Boston, MA * Type: Chrome * Postmark: Not Used * Value Index: C

When the Brooklyn Dodgers decided to move to Los Angeles, Walter O'Malley, the owner, had three choices for a place to play while their stadium was being built. They could use the 20,000-seat Wrigley Field (a Minor League field) the 100,000-seat Rose Bowl in Pasadena (a few miles from Los Angeles) or the Los Angeles Coliseum. O'Malley chose the Coliseum which had 80,000 more seats than Wrigley Field. The Coliseum was used primarily for football and the Baseball configuration would have to be adjusted to the dimensions of the stadium. The seats in left field were only 250 feet from home plate and a 42-foot screen extending 140 feet to left center field had to be erected. The distance to right field was 301 feet down the foul line, and 440 feet to center field. This photograph was taken during the Dodger's first season at the Coliseum.

This photograph was taken on May 7, 1959 at the Los Angeles Coliseum and shows the largest crowd in the history of major league Baseball. The event was not a regular season game as 93,103 fans filled the Coliseum to honor Dodger catcher Roy Campanella who had been paralyzed in an automobile accident. The Dodgers played the Yankees in this exhibition game with the proceeds going to help pay Roy's huge hospital expenses. The demand for tickets was very large, to the extent that 15,000 fans were turned away because the Coliseum was filled to capacity. This photograph was taken from a high position in the left center field seats. It shows the closeness of the left field stands to home plate, only 250 feet. It also shows the vast space in right

Publisher: Souvenir Color Card Company, Los Angeles, CA, Card No. LA1126 * Manufacturer: H.S. Crocker Company, Los Angeles, CA * Type: Chrome * Postmark: Not Used * Value Index: C

center field where a 440-foot HR is required to clear the fence. With the trend to smaller Baseball parks today with a capacity of 50,000 persons we can assume a crowd of this size will not be topped.

Among the Major League Baseball players born in Cuba, outfielder Orestes "Minnie" Minoso ranks as one of the best. Although he relied more on speed than power, Minoso had 100 RBI four times during his career, led the League in stolen bases three times, was the leader in triples three times, and led in doubles once. As a skilled defensive outfielder he could run and catch fly balls that other players could not reach. Minoso began playing Baseball with the Indians in 1949 and played in 9 games. After being sent to the Minor Leagues for one year he joined the Indians in 1951. He was then traded to the White Sox, after playing 8 games. He became an immediate star for the White Sox with a .321 BA and was an outstanding player for the remainder of his career.

Publisher: George Brace Photo, Chicago, IL * Manufacturer: Not Indicated * Type: Chrome * Postmark: Not Used * Value Index: B

Carl Furillo played his entire 15-year Major League career with the Dodgers. He was an important factor in the success of the team from 1946, when he joined the Dodgers, until he retired in 1960. The right-fielder was an example of consistency with an overall .299 BA and a reputation for the strongest throwing arm in Baseball. Furillo was nicknamed the "Reading Rifle" because of his ability to "gun down" base runners with his accurate throws.

Carl's finest season came in 1953 when he led the National League with a .344 BA and 92 RBI to lead the Dodgers to a Pennant. His amazing hitting continued in the World Series with 8 hits in 24 times at bat for a .333 BA. Despite his efforts the Dodgers lost to the Yankees four games to two. His career high was 106 RBI in 1949 and 1950. Furillo was outstanding at fielding balls that bounced off the Right Field wall and catching runners trying to stretch a single into a double. When the Dodgers left for Los Angeles in 1958, Furillo was 36 years old and nearing to the end of his career. Carl had a .290 BA and led the team with 83 RBI during his first season in Los Angeles. This photograph was taken in 1959 as he played on his final Pennant-winning team.

Publisher: Los Angeles Dodgers, Los Angeles, CA, Card No. LA-D-904 * Manufacturer: H.S. Crocker Company, Inc., Los Angeles, CA * Type: Chrome * Postmark: Not Used * Value Index: C

Some players save their best efforts for the big moments and Dodger pitcher Johnny Podres is an example. The lefthanded pitcher joined the Dodgers in 1953 and won 9 and lost 4 games in his rookie season. During that year he also lost his only World Series appearance to the Yankees. From that moment on, Podres never lost another Worlds Series game finishing with 4 wins and 1 loss. Using 1955 as an example, he had a record of 9 wins and 10 losses going into the World Series where he pitched superb games against the Yankees pitching 9 innings for an 8 to 3 win in game No. 3 and a 5 to 0 shutout in the seventh and deciding game. He allowed only 5 hits and gave the Dodgers their only World Championship in Brooklyn. This photograph was taken in 1959 when Podres had a regular season record of 14 wins and 9 losses and won his only World Series appearance in the sixth and deciding game.

Publisher: Los Angeles Dodgers, Los Angeles, CA, Card No. LA-D-903 * Manufacturer: H.S. Crocker Company, Inc., Los Angeles, CA * Type: Chrome * Postmark: Not Used * Value Index: C

Lefthander Billy Pierce began his major league career with his home town Detroit Tigers in 1945 and was traded to the Chicago White Sox in 1949 where he won 7 and lost 15 games for a sixth-place club. This photograph was taken at Yankee Stadium in 1955 when Pierce was a 15-game winner for the third place White Sox.

While pitching for teams that often finished in the Second Division, he won 211 against 169 losses before retiring in 1964.

He had two 20 victory seasons for the White Sox in 1956 and 1957. They were 12 games behind the Yankees in 1956 and 8 games behind the Yankees in 1957. In the 1959 World Series against the Dodgers he pitched 4 innings in relief, allowing no runs on 2 hits, walking 2, and striking out 3 batters to record a perfect 0.00 ERA. Traditionally the White Sox have been a light hitting club and one may wonder at the number of victories he might have had if there had been stronger batting support.

Publisher: Louis Dormand, Riverhead, NY, Card No. 1907 * Manufacturer: Not Indicated * Type: Chrome: * Postmark: Not Used * Value Index: C

When the Chicago White Sox won the Pennant in 1959 they were referred to as the "Go-Go Sox" because of their speed and daring on the bases and their superb defensive ability. Second baseman Nellie Fox was the personification of the go-go spirit. He was the example of this spirit, but not for stolen bases as he had only five in 1959. He was able to ignite rallies by getting on base, driving in key runs, and ending the opponent rallies with remarkable fielding. Fox led the 1959 White Sox with a .306 BA and was second with 70 RBI to catcher Sherman Lollar's 84 RBI. The quick fielding of Fox led all of the American League second basemen in putouts and assists, forming a superb double play combination with shortstop Luis Aparicio. That year he was rewarded with the Most Valuable Player award. In the World Series he had a .375 BA on 9 hits in 24 times at bat. Despite these heroics the Dodgers won, four games to two. Four times in his 19-year career he led the League in BHs and compiled a career .283 BA. Baseball authorities, including Ted Williams, have publicly stated that Fox belongs in the Hall of Fame.

Publisher: Nellie Fox Bowl, Chambersburg, PA * Manufacturer: Not Indicated * Type: Black & White * Postmark: Not Used * Value Index: B

Duke Snider had been a member of the Dodgers for 12 years when this photograph was taken in 1959. He led the Dodgers with a .308 BA and 88 RBI. Snider was a big factor in the Dodgers winning the 1959 Pennant. He became as popular in Los Angeles as in Brooklyn. His popularity began when he joined the Dodgers as a 21-year old outfielder in 1947. Snider's finest season was in 1955 with 42 HRs, 126 runs scored, 136 RBI, and a .309 BA. They won the Pennant and defeated the Yankees four games to three in the World Series. He liked Brooklyn but was very happy with the move to California, as he was born in Los Angeles and had his off-season home there.

Publisher: Los Angeles Dodgers, Los Angeles, CA, Card No. LA-D-901 * Manufacturer: H.S. Crocker Company, Los Angeles, CA * Type: Chrome * Postmark: Not Used * Value Index: C

Righthander Don Drysdale was the ace pitcher of the Dodgers' 1959 staff. He began his career with the team in 1956 in Brooklyn. The move to California delighted him as he was born in Van Nuys, California. Drysdale standing 6-feet-5-inches tall was a forbidding figure on the pitching mound with his height, blazing fast ball, and excellent pitching control. In this Pennant winning season "Big D" struck out 242 batters to lead the National League. His 17 wins led the Dodgers during the regular season and he won his World Series game by a 3 to 1 score. This photograph of Drysdale is part of a 12-Postcard set issued by he Dodgers. This picture was the only one not taken at the Los Angeles Coliseum as he was not available when the photographs were taken. His photograph was taken later at Wrigley Field, former home of the Pacific Coast League Los Angeles Angels where the Dodgers practiced on occasion.

Publisher: Los Angeles Dodgers, Los Angeles, CA, Card No. LA-D-905 * Manufacturer: H.S. Crocker Company, Los Angeles, CA * Type: Chrome * Postmark: Not Used * Value Index: B

Sanford "Sandy" Koufax was one of only a few players who was able to sign a contract with his hometown team. In 1954 he signed a $14,000 bonus contract with the Dodgers. Surprisingly, he did not play Baseball with his high school team until his senior year. Koufax was an outstanding basketball player and won a basketball scholarship to the University of Cincinnati where he also played Baseball and attracted the attention of the major league scouts because of his fast ball. During his freshman year he struck out 51 batters in only 32 innings. During the Summer he played sandlot baseball for the Parkviews in a Coney Island League. In September 1954 he worked out at Ebbets Field and was offered a contract and a place on the 1955 team. Koufax was one of the few players who did not play in the minor leagues. Sandy was not an immediate success as he lacked fast-ball control. During his first six seasons he won 36 and lost 40 games. He developed into a star in 1961, winning 18 and losing 13 games and set a League record with 269 strikeouts, surpassing the record of 267 strikeouts by the Giants' Christy Mathewson in 1903. During the next six years he was Baseball's dominant pitcher winning 136 games. In 1966 he had to retire from Baseball due to arthritis in his left elbow.

Publisher: Los Angeles Dodgers, Los Angeles, CA, Card No. LA-D-906 * Manufacturer H.S. Crocker, Los Angeles, CA * Type: Chrome * Postmark: Not Used * Value Index: B

Cover Design by Joseph Mastrantuono
Book Design and layout by Milton Martir
This book is set in 10 points Berkeley Medium,
with 12 points of lead,
with display type in Berkeley Bold.

BIBLIOGRAPHY

Allen, Lee, COOPERSTOWN CORNER, Ohio: Society for American Baseball Research, 1990

Allen, Lee, THE CINCINNATI REDS, New York: G.P. Putnam & Sons, 1948

Allen, Lee, THE WORLD SERIES, New York: G.P. Putnam & Sons, 1969

American League of Professional Baseball Clubs, AMERICAN LEAGUE REDBOOK,

American Sports Publishing Company, SPALDING BASEBALL GUIDE,

Barber, Red, THE BROADCASTERS, New York: The Dial Press, 1970

Bealle, Morris, THE WASHINGTON SENATORS, Washington, DC: Columbia Publishing Co., 1947

Boudreau, Lou and Ed Fitzgerald, PLAYER MANAGER, Massachusetts: Little, Brown & Co., 1948

Bready, James H., THE HOME TEAM, Maryland: James H. Bready, 1971

Broeg, Bob, SUPERSTARS OF BASEBALL, Missouri: The Sporting News, 1971

Brown, Warren, THE CHICAGO CUBS, New York: G.P. Putnam & Sons, 1946

Brown, Warren, THE CHICAGO WHITE SOX, New York: G.P. Putnam & Sons, 1952

Butler, Hal, THE HARMON KILLEBREW STORY, New York: Julian Messner, 1966

Cox, James, THE LIVELY BALL, Virginia: Redefinition, 1989

Danzig, Allison and Joe Reichler, THE HISTORY OF BASEBALL, New Jersey: Prentice-Hall, 1959

Detroit Baseball Co., DETROIT IN BASEBALL, Michigan: 1939

Dickson, Paul, THE DICKSON BASEBALL DICTIONARY, New York: Facts On File, 1989

Durso, Joseph, YANKEE STADIUM, Massachusetts: Houghton-Mifflin Co., 1972

Ellis, William T., BILLY SUNDAY, THE MAN AND HIS MESSAGE, Pennsylvania: The John C. Winston Co., 1917

Feller, Bob, STRIKEOUT STORY, New York: A.S. Barnes & Co., 1947

Frankenberg, T.T., BILLY SUNDAY, HIS TABERNACLES AND SAWDUST TRAILS, Ohio: F.J. Heer Printing Co., 1917

Goudy, Curt, COWBOY AT THE MIKE, New York: Doubleday & Co., 1966

Graham, Frank, McGRAW OF THE GIANTS, New York: G.P. Putnam & Sons, 1944

Graham, Frank, THE BROOKLYN DODGERS, New York: G.P. Putnam & Sons, 1948

Guilfoile, Bill, NATIONAL BASEBALL HALL OF FAME AND MUSEUM YEARBOOK, New York: 1989

Jedick, Peter, LEAGUE PARK, Ohio: Jedick, 1978

Kaese, Harold & R.G. Lynch, THE MILWAUKEE BRAVES: New York: G.P. Putnam's & Sons, 1954

Lewis, Franklin, THE CLEVELAND INDIANS, New York: G.P. Putnam & Sons, 1949

Lieb, Frederick G., THE DETROIT TIGERS, New York: G.P. Putnam & Sons, 1946

Lieb, Frederick G., THE PITTSBURGH PIRATES, New York: G.P. Putnam's & Sons, 1946

Lieb, Frederick G., THE ST. LOUIS CARDINALS, New York: G.P. Putnam & Sons, 1945

Lieb, Frederick G., THE WORLD SERIES, New York: G.P. Putnam & Sons, 1945

Lieb, Frederick G. & Stan Baumgartner, THE PHILADELPHIA PHILLIES, New York: G.P. Putnam's & Sons, 1953

Lowry, Philip J., GREEN CATHEDRALS, New York: SABR, 1986

Mack, Connie, MY 66 YEARS IN BASEBALL, Pennsylvania: Universal House, 1950

Mann, Arthur, BRANCH RICKEY, AMERICAN IN ACTION, Massachusetts: Houghton-Mifflin Co., 1957

Mann, Arthur, THE REAL McGRAW, New York: David McKay Co., 1953

McGraw, John, MY THIRTY YEARS IN BASEBALL, New York: Boni & Liveright, 1923

Meade, William B., EVEN THE BROWNS, Illinois: Contemporary Books, Inc., 1978

Meany, Tom, MILWAUKEE'S MIRACLE BRAVES, New York: A.S. Barnes & Co., 1954

Mehl, Ernest, THE KANSAS CITY ATHLETICS, New York: Henry Holt & Co., 1956

Mitchell, Jerry, SANDY KOUFAX, New York: Grossett & Dunlap, 1966

National League of Professional Baseball Clubs, NATIONAL LEAGUE GREEN BOOK, New York: Jay Publishing Co., 1991

National League of Professional Baseball Clubs, OFFICIAL NATIONAL LEAGUE HISTORY, New York: Jay Publishing Co., 1950

Povich, Shirley, THE WASHINGTON SENATORS, New York: G.P. Putnam & Sons, 1954

Reach, A.J., REACH OFFICAL AMERICAN LEAGUE BASEBALL GUIDE, Pennsylvania:, 1916

Reidenbaugh, Lowell, TAKE ME OUT TO THE BALL PARK, Missouri: The Sporting News, 1983

Romig, Ralph H., CY YOUNG, Pennsylvania: Dorrance & Co. 1964

Shannon, Bill and Gary Kalinsky, THE BALLPARKS, New York: Hawthorn, 1975

Smith, Ira, BASEBALL'S FAMOUS FIRST BASEMEN, New York: A.S. Barnes & Co., 1956

Smith, Ira, BASEBALL'S FAMOUS PITCHERS, New York: A.S. Barnes & Co., 1954

Smith, Ken, BASEBALL'S HALL OF FAME, New York: A.S. Barnes & Co., 1947

Smith, Robert, BASEBALL, New York: Simon & Schuster, 1947

Spink, H.G. Taylor, OFFICIAL BASEBALL GUIDE, Missouri: The Sporting News 19

Treat, Roger L., WALTER JOHNSON, KING OF THE PITCHERS, New York: Julian Messner, 1948

Trimble, Joe, PHIL RIZZUTO, New York: A.S. Barnes & Co., 1951

Williams, Ted and John Underwood, MY TURN AT BAT, New York: Simon & Schuster, 1969

Zimmerman, Paul, THE LOS ANGELES DODGERS, New York: Coward- McCann, 1960

Index

A

A.G. Spalding & Bros., 26, 27, 29
Aaron, Hank, 105, 114
Aaron, Tommie, 105
Adams, Franklin P., 15
Aldrige, Vic, 58
Alexander, Grover Cleveland, 47, 59, 77, 115
All Star Game, 37, 65
All Stars, 67
Allegheny River, 4, 6
Allen, Lee, 97
Allen, Mel, 100
Alston Golf Course, 46
Altrock, Nick, 11
American Association, 3, 7, 59
American League, 1, 2, 3, 4, 8, 9, 11, 12, 16, 17, 19,
    22, 24, 28, 31, 33, 36, 38, 44, 46, 54, 57, 61, 62,
    65, 67, 68, 71, 72, 78, 81, 82, 87, 92, 96, 97, 98,
    102, 104, 106, 107, 108, 109, 111, 116
American League Orioles, 10 (Also see Orioles)
American League's Boston Puritans, 7 (Also see
    Puritans)
American League's first Negro ball player, 89
Ames, Red, 9
Aparcio, Luis, 121
Arlin, Harold W., 53
Athletics, 2, 24, 27, 109, 110 (Also see Kansas City
    Athletics and Philadelphia Athletics)
Atlanta, GA, 34
Atlantic Avenue Depot of the Long Island Railroad,
    113
Averill, Earl, 65, 72

B

B.F. Goodrich Tires, 69
Baker Bowl, 47, 109
Baker, Frank "Home Run", 31, 33, 37
Baker, William F., 47 2
Baltimore, 2, 4, 43, 44, 71, 109
Baltimore Elite Giants, 116
Baltimore Orioles, 1, 4, 6, 7, 8, 10, 12, 29, 52, 55, 97
    (Also see Orioles and American League Orioles)
Baltimore Terrapins, 43, 44
Barber, Red, 53

Barnhart, Clyde, 58
Barrow, Ed, 86, 96
Barry, Jack, 31, 33
Bartell, Dick, 65
Baseball Advertising Postcards, 110
Baseball Guide, 29
Baseball Hall of Fame, 8, 10, 13, 15, 17, 19, 74, 82,
    97, 101 (Also see Hall of Fame)
Baseball Museum, 77
Baseball Reserve Clause, 43
Baseball Writers of America, 77
"Baseball's Sad Lexicon", 15
Bel Geddes, Norman, 113
Bell, Les, 59
Bender, Chief, 9, 33
Bennett, Charley, 3, 47
Bennett, James Gordon, 5
Bennett Park, 3, 37
Bentley, Jack, 55
Berger, Walley, 65
Berra, Lawrence Peter "Yogi", 106, 108, 116
Bickford, Vern, 89
"Big Bear", 107
"Big D", 122
"Black Hand", 20
"Black Sox", 48
"Black Sox Scandal", 48
Blazing Fastball, 102
Bluege, Ossie, 111
Blues, 8
Blues Stadium, 109
"Bonehead", 21
Borchert Field, 98
Borowy, Hank, 81
Boston, 1, 3, 4, 6, 10, 24, 66, 71, 76, 78, 81
Boston Beaneaters, 7
Boston Braves, 10, 65, 72, 89, 90, 91, 98, 103 (Also
    see Braves)
Boston Celtics, 114
Boston Puritans (Red Sox), 1, 2, 6, 7, 24, 34, 39, 40,
    41, 47, 52, 54, 65, 81, 85, 90, 92, 111, 112
Boston Red Stockings, 3, 26
Boston University Athletic Department, 46
Boston's Fenway Park, 92
Boston's Huntington Avenue Grounds, 7

Bottomley, Sunny Jim, 59
Boudreau, Lou, 89, 90, 107
Bowman, Joe, 68
Bradenton, FL, 98, 114, 116
Braves, 45, 71, 75, 76, 100 (See Milwaukee Braves)
Braves Field, 30, 45, 46, 86, 98
Breadon, Sam, 60
Brecheen, Harry "The Cat", 85
Bresnahan, Roger, 6, 9
Bressler, Rube, 16
Bridges, Tommie, 68, 69
Bridwell, Al, 21, 29
Briggs Stadium, 68, 82, 87
Briggs, Walter, 87
Broncos, 8
"Bronx Bombers", 61, 79, 101
Brooklyn, 43, 44, 51, 52, 66, 72, 117, 120, 122
Brooklyn Dodgers, 1, 22, 41, 51, 52, 65, 71, 87, 96, 106, 107, 118 (Also see Dodgers and Los Angeles Dodgers)
Brooklyn Superbas, 4
Brotherhood Park, 5
Brown, Mordecai "Three Finger", 10, 19, 20
Browns, 71, 82
Brush, John T., 7, 9, 36
Brush Stadium, 36
"Bullet Bob", 104
Bush, Joe, 39

C

Campanella, Roy, 116, 119
Canadians, 103
Cardinals, 67, 81, 82, 88 (Also see National League Cardinals)
Carey, Max, 58
Carnegie, Andrew, 24
Caveretta, Phil, 81
CBS Radio "Game of the Week", 97
Centennial of Baseball, 73
Century of Progress, 65 (Also see Worlds Fair)
"Chairman of the Board", 101
Champman, Ray, 51
Chance, Frank L., 10, 15, 19, 20, 27
Chapman, Ben, 65
Chapman, Jack, 12
Cherokee Indian, 102
Chesterfield Cigarettes, 97
Cheyenne, WY, 100
Chicago, 4, 19, 43, 71
Chicago Colts, 46
Chicago Cubs, 10, 11, 13, 15, 20, 21, 31, 40, 43, 63, 65, 69, 78, 79, 81, 82, 90 (Also see Cubs)

Chicago, IL, 79
Chicago Tribune, 65
Chicago Wanderers Cricket Club, 30
Chicago Whales, 60, 79
Chicago White Sox, 11, 13, 38, 40, 48, 49, 50, 54, 65, 92, 95, 98, 102, 104, 108, 121 (Also see White Sox)
Chicago White Stockings, 26, 47
Chrysler Corporation, 69
Cicotte, Eddie, 48
Cincinnati, 73, 75, 81, 86
Cincinnati Baseball Grounds, 12
Cincinnati Red Stockings, 24
Cincinnati Reds, 17, 48, 49, 65, 68, 72, 75, 76, 80, 81
Cincinnati, 38
Clark, Stephen C., 74, 77
Clarke, Fred, 7
Cleveland, 4, 8, 29, 30, 31, 37, 43, 51, 52, 72, 95, 107, 118
Cleveland Indians, 51, 65, 85, 88, 89, 91, 102, 103, 104, 106, 107
Cleveland League Park, 3
Cleveland Municipal Stadium, 61, 62
Cleveland Naps, 37
Cleveland, OH, 56
Cleveland Spiders, 3, 24
Coakley, Andy, 9
Cobb, Ty, 16, 17, 19, 22, 28, 37, 77, 94
Cochrane, Mickey, 68, 69
Cohan, George M., 58
Cole Aero Eight Automobiles, 55
Collins, Eddie, 31, 33, 37, 77
Collins, Rip, 69
Colonial Motel, 110
Columbia Park, 2, 22
Columbian Exposition, 1893, 11
Comiskey, Charles A., 11, 30, 38, 48, 50
Comiskey Park, 30, 43, 50, 65
Comstock, C.B., 44
Conley, Gene, 114
Conlin, Mike, 9
Connie Mack Stadium, 95, 109
Cooley, Duff, 1
Coombs, Jack, 31, 33
Cooper, Mort, 82
Cooper, Walker, 82, 83
Cooperstown, NY, 73, 74, 77
County Stadium, 98, 99, 113
Covington, Kentucky, 43
Cowan, Thomas, 53
Cowboy At The Mike, 100
Crandall, Del, 116
Crawford, Sam, 17, 28, 37

Cronin, Joe, 65
Crosley Field, 68, 72, 73, 87
Crowder, Alvin, 65
Crowder, General, 62
Cuba, 38
Cubs, 13, 19, 27, 60 (Also see Chicago Cubs)
Cuccinello, Tony, 65
Cullenbine, Roy, 79
Cuyler, Kiki, 58, 60
Cy Young Award, 24 (Also see Young, Cy)

D

Dahlen, Bill, 7, 10
Danning, Harry, 76
Daper, Cliff, 97
Daubert, Jake, 52
Davis, Harry, 9, 31, 33, 36
Davis, Zachary Taylor, 30, 43
Dean, Daffy, 69
Dean, Dizzy, 69, 88
Delahanty, Ed, 17
Derringer, Paul, 68, 73, 75, 81, 97
Detroit, 4, 16, 31, 32, 57, 69, 77, 82
Detroit Tigers, 8, 12, 16, 17, 19, 22, 28, 37, 57, 65, 69, 72, 73, 75, 77, 87, 98, 109, 111, 121
Detroit Wolverines, 3, 47
Devery, Bill, 4, 38
Devlin, Art, 20
Dexter Portland Cement, 27
Dickey, Bill, 65
DiMaggio, Dom, 81
DiMaggio, Vince, 81
Dimaggio, Yankee Clipper Joe, 79, 81, 102, 112
Ditmar, Art, 110
Doby, Larry, 89, 104
Dodge, 69
Dodger, 119
Dodgers, 44, 52, 75, 83, 106, 113, 115, 117, 120, 121, 122 (Also see Brooklyn Dodgers and Los Angeles Dodgers)
Donatelli, Augie, 97
Donlin, Mike, 2
Donovan, Wild Bill, 19, 22
Doubleday, General Abner, 73, 74
Dreyfuss, Barney, 7, 24
Drysdale, Don, 122
Dudley, Jimmy, 88
Dugan, Joe, 39
Dugout Lounge, 112
Dunn, Jack, 7, 55
Durocher, Leo, 72
Durocher, Lippy, 69

Dykes, Jimmy, 61, 65

E

Earl Mann's Atlanta Crackers of the Southern Association 97
Ebbets, Charley, 41
Ebbets Field, 22, 30, 41, 52, 72, 73, 113, 115, 122
"ee-yah", 12
Egypt, PA, 94
Electric Scoreboards, 51
Elite Postcard Shop, 34
Eller, Hod, 72
Ellis, Dr. William T., 47
Empire State Building, 83
English, Woody, 65
Ennis, Del, 95
Evers, Johnny, 10, 15, 21
Exposition Park, 4, 6, 24, 26

F

Farrell, Frank, 4, 38
Farrell, Rick, 65
Farrell, Wes, 65
Federal League, 22, 30, 43, 44, 60, 79
Federal League Rebels, 6
Feller, Bob, 88, 91
Feller, "Rapid" Roger, 72
Felsch, Happy, 48
Fenway Park, 30, 39, 41, 45, 66, 93
Ferriss, Boo, 85
"First Full-Time Radio Announcer In The World", 53
"First In War, First In Peace and Last in the American League", 96
Fisherman's Wharf, 81
Forbes Field, 26, 27, 30, 53, 58
Ford, Whitey, 101
Fox, Nellie, 121
Fox, Peter, 68
Foxx, Jimmy, 61, 65
Frazee, Harry, 39
Fresno, CA, 19
Frick, Ford, 77
Frisch, Fordham Flash, 69
Frisch, Frankie, 65
Fullerton, Hugh, 32
Furillo, Carl, 120

G

Gandil, Chick, 48
Garagiola, Joe, 108
Garcia, Mike, 107
"Gas House Gang", 67

Gehrig, Lou, 57, 60, 63, 65
Gehringer, Charley, 65, 68
Geiser, Jack, 30
"Georgia Peach", 16
Gettysburg College, 33
Giants, 5, 33, 39, 54, 55, 66, 71, 75, 76, 83 (Also see
 New York Giants)
Gilmore,James A., 43
Girard College, 36
"Go-Go-Sox", 121
Gomex, Lefty, 63, 65
Gordon Highlanders, 4
Gordon, Joe, 79
Gordon, John W., 4
Gowdy, Curt, 100
Graham, Charles, Jr., 117
Graney, Jack, 88, 90
Grantland Rice, 53
Graves, Abner, 74
Gray, Dolly, 35
Great Depression, 68
"Green Monster", 66, 93
Greenberg, Hank, 68, 82
Greenfield Cafeteria and Coffee Shop, 69
Griffith, Clark, 39, 57, 111
Griffith Stadium, 96, 112
Grimm, Charley, 81
Grove, Lefty, 62, 65
"Gun Down", 120

H

Hack, Stan, 81   3
Hafey, Chick, 60, 65
Haines, Pop, 69
Hall of Fame, 6, 28, 29, 33, 40, 44, 49, 54, 66, 69, 73,
 76, 77, 85, 88, 90, 94, 97, 103, 107, 108, 111, 112,
 116, 121 (Also see Baseball Hall of Fame)
Hall-of-Famer, 17, 31, 33
Hallahan, Wild Bill, 65
Hamilton, OH, 80
Harder, Mel, 62
Harlem River, 56, 63
Harridge, Will, 77
Harris, Stanley "Bucky", 57, 96
Harrison Park, 44
Hartnett, Gabby, 65
Hartsell, Topsy, 31
Harvel, IL, 54
Harwell, Ernie, 97, Introduction
Haymaker, Troy, 5
Hayworth, Ray, 68
"Heart-breakers", 104

Heilman, Harry, 57
Herman, George, 56
Hershberger, Willard, 76
Highlanders, 4, 10, 44
Hildebrand, Oral, 65
Hilltop Park, 4, 38
Hornsby, Roger, 60
Hoyt, Waite, 39, 57
Hubbell, Carl, 65
Huggins, Miller, 17
Hughson, Tex, 85
Hunt, Sandy, 53
"Husk", 19

I

Indianapolis, 43
Indianapolis Champions, 44
Indianapolis Club of the American Association, 40
Indians, 61, 62, 107, 119
International League, 55
"Iron Man", 8
Irvington, CA, 19
Island Railroad, 113

J

Jackson, Shoeless Joe, 35, 48
Japan, 67
Jennings, Hughie, 12, 19, 44
Johnson, Arnold, 109
Johnson, Ban, 4, 38
Johnson, Don, 81
Johnson, Walter, 37, 38, 46, 77, 96, 115
Joss, Addie, 37
"Junk ball", 102
"Jury Box", 86

K

Kaese, Harold, 45
Kansas City, 27, 43, 71, 109 (Also see Athletics)
Kansas City Athletics, 90, 112
Kansas City Blues in the American Association, 109
Kansas City, KS, 110
Kansas City Monarchs of the Negro National League   3
Kansas City Municipal Stadium, 110
Karsans, Armando, 38
Kaufman, Al, 1
KDKA, 53
Keeler, Wee Willie, 44, 77
Keelty, James, Jr., 104
Kell, George, 111
Keller, Charley, 79
Kelley, Joe, 44

Kellner, Alex, 110
Kellogg Company, 83
Kellogg Postcards, 83
KFBC, 100
Killea, Harry, 7
Killebrew, Harmon, 111
Kiner, Ralph, 83, 85
"King Carl", 65
"King of Swat", 67
"King of the Base Stealers", 115
Klein, Chuck, 65
Kling, Johnny, 19
Klinger, Bob, 85
Knabe, Otto, 43
KOMA, 100
Korea, 78
Koufax, Sanford "Sandy", 122
Kramer, Jack, 82
Kremer, Ray, 58
Krevich, Mike, 82
Kubrick, Al, 1

L

Lajoie, Napoleon, 2, 8, 37, 77
Lake Erie, 62, 91
Landis, Kenesaw Mountain, 48, 77
Lapp, Jack, 31
Lazzeri, Tony, 57, 65
Leach, Tommy, 1, 26
League Park, 31, 37, 51, 62
Lemon, Bob, 107, 108
Lieb, Fred, 118
Lincoln Street, 21
Little Napoleon, 58
Lollar, Sherman, 121
Lombardi, Ernie, 75, 76
Lopat, Ed, 102
Lopez, Al, 106
Lord, Bristol, 31
Los Angeles, 41, 117, 118, 120, 122
Los Angeles Coliseum, 118, 119, 122
Los Angeles Dodgers, 71, 88, 115 (Also see Brooklyn
   Dodgers and Dodgers)
Louisville, 1, 12
Louisville Colonels, 10
Lundgren, Carl, 19

M

Mack, Connie, 2, 9, 22, 31, 33, 36, 61, 62, 65, 67, 87,
   109
MacPhail, Larry, 68, 86, 87
Mantle, Mickey, 98, 111, 112

Marion, Marty, 82
Maris, Roger, 57
Marquard, Rube, 40, 52
Marshall, Willard, 83
Martin, Pepper, 65, 69
Maryland, 55
Mathews, Eddie, 114
Mathewson, Christy, 5, 6, 7, 8, 9, 20, 33, 41, 52, 77,
   115, 122
Mays, Carl, 39, 51
Mays, Willie, 118
McCormick, Frank, 76
McCormick, Harry, 21
McGann, Dan, 10
McGinnis, Stuffy, 58
McGinnity, "Iron Man" Joe, 1, 6, 7, 8, 9, 33, 52
McGowan, Bill, 97
McGraw, John, 1, 6, 8, 10, 13, 21, 29, 36, 40, 44, 52,
   54, 56, 58, 65
McGuire, Jack, 108
McKechnie, Bill, 58, 60, 73, 76
McKeever, Ed, 41
McKeever, Steve, 41
McMullin, Fred, 48
McNamee, Graham, 53
Meadows, Lee, 58
Medwick, Ducky, 69
Medwick, Joe, 101
Meer, Johnny Vander, 72
Memorial Stadium, 104, 105
Merkle, Fred, 21
Mertes, Sam, 10
Metropolitans, 5
Michigan State University, 94
Miles, Clarence W., 104
Miller, Bing, 61
Milwaukee, 4, 71
Milwaukee Braves, 113, 114 (Also see Braves)
Milwaukee Brewers of the American Association, 98
Milwaukee County Stadium, 99, 100, 105
Minor League Brewers, 98
Minoso, Orestes "Minnie", 119
Mize, Big Cat, 70
Mize, Johnny, 70, 83, 101
Monogahela River, 6
Montreal Royals of the International League, 87
Moore, Terry, 82
Morrison, Johnny, 58
Most Valuable Player, 106, 116, 118
Most Valuable Player Award, 76, 96, 121
Mullin, George, 28
Muncipal Stadium, 31, 72, 88, 91, 100, 103

"Murderers Row", 57
Murphy, Danny, 31
Musial, "Stan The Man", 82
MY 66 YEARS IN THE BIG LEAGUES, 2, 33
MY THIRTY YEARS IN BASEBALL, 8, 9, 13, 40
MY TURN AT BAT, 78

N

Naps, 8
National Association, 26
National Baketball Association, 114
National League, 1, 2, 3, 5, 6, 7, 8, 10, 11, 12, 13, 17,
    20, 21, 22, 24, 26, 29, 38, 40, 44, 49, 58, 59, 60,
    63, 65, 66, 68, 71, 75, 77, 80, 81, 83, 85, 87, 89,
    93, 95, 97, 99, 100, 103, 104, 105, 107, 109, 114,
    116, 120
National League Cardinals, 67 (Also see Cardinals)
National League Phillies, 2 (Also see Philadelphia
    Phillies)
National League Spiders, 30 (Also see Spiders)
Navin Field, 37
Navin, Frank, 37
Negro (as a black or Afro-American was designated), 3
Negro National League, 89, 105, 116
New League Park, 30
New Polo Grounds, 30
New York, 32, 60, 81
New York Evening Mail, 15
New York Giants, 6, 7, 8, 9, 10, 11, 15, 20, 21, 29,
    33, 40, 41, 49, 52, 53, 54, 56, 57, 58, 60, 63, 65,
    71, 83, 96, 97, 107, 117 (Also see Giants)
New York Highlanders, 11, 22, 33, 38, 46   2
New York Mets, 85, 108
New York, NY, 56
New York Times, 56
New York Tribune, 53
New York Yankees, 17, 51, 52, 59, 65, 81, 86, 96,
    100, 101, 102, 103, 104, 106, 108, 112 (Also see
    Yankees)
Newark Call, 53
Newark Eagles, 89
Newark, NJ, 44, 53
Newhouser, Hal, 82
Newsome, Bobo, 72
Nichols, Kid, 3
Night Baseball, 68, 86, 87
Nixon, Richard, 35
Noyes Buick, 93
Noyes, Tom, 34
Nuxhall, Joe, 80

O

O'Day, Hank, 21

O'Doul, Lefty, 65, 66
Oklahoma City, 100
Oklahoma City Indians of the Texas League, 100
Oldring, Rube, 31
O'Loughlin, Silk, 41
O'Malley, Walter, 113, 115, 118
Orioles, 8, 44, 71, 104, 111 (Also see American
    League Orioles)
Osborn Engineering Company, 56, 66
Ott, Mel, 71
Overall, Orval, 13
Overall, Orvie, 19
Owen, Frank, 11

P

Pacific Coast League, 66
Pafko, Andy, 79, 81
"Paint Account", 86
"Palace of the Fans", 11, 12, 38
Parkviews in a Coney Island League, 122
Passeau, Claude, 81
Peckinpaugh, Roger, 62
"Peerless Leader", 10, 19, 27
Pennock, Herb, 39
Pennsylvania Dairy Council, 94
Peppers Park, 44
Perini Brothers, 98, 99
Perini, Lou, 86
Pfeffer, Jeff, 52
Pfeister, Jack, 19, 20
Pfeister, Jake, 10
Philadelphia, 1, 2, 4, 22, 24, 27, 33, 36, 71, 81
Philadelphia Athletics, 5, 9, 16, 22, 24, 28, 31, 33, 36,
    60, 61, 62, 65, 75, 98, 109, 111 (Also see Athletics)
Philadelphia Phillies, 43, 47, 53, 65, 68, 94, 95, 101,
    109 (Also see National League Phillies)
Phillies, 27, 66, 71, 94, 109
Phillippe, Deacon, 6, 7
Pierce, Billy, 121
Pirates, 6, 7, 26
Pittsburgh, 6, 7, 26, 24, 43, 53, 57, 81
Pittsburgh Pirates, 1, 2, 4, 9, 22, 24, 28, 47, 53, 57,
    58, 60, 83, 85, 104
Plank, Eddie, 9, 33
PLAYER MANAGER, 90
Players League, 5
Podres, Johnny, 120
Polk Street, 21
Polo Grounds, 5, 20, 21, 26, 36, 38, 55, 56, 63, 65,
    71, 76, 94, 97, 117, 118
Postage Stamp, 73
Potter, Nelson, 82
Power, Vic, 110

Pulliam, Harry, 21
Puritans, 7, 9, 24 (Also see American League's Boston Puritans)
Putnam, George, 117

Q

Quinn, Bob, 66

R

Radio Corporation of America (RCA), 53
Radiola 46, 53
"Rapid Robert", 88
REACH GUIDE, 24
"Reading Rifle", 120
Red Sox, 1, 7, 39, 45, 66, 71
Redland Field, 11, 12, 38, 48
Reds, 11, 12, 73, 75
Reese, Harold "Pee Wee", 106
Reulbach, Ed, 10, 19
Reynolds, Allie, 102
Rhem, Flint, 59
Richey, Branch, 97
Richmond Hills High School, 96
Rickey, Branch, 87
"Riding", 86
Riggs, Lew, 72
Risberg, Swede, 48
Rizzuto, Phil, 96
Roberts, Robin, 94
Robinson, Brooks, 111
Robinson, Jackie, 87, 89, 106, 115
Robinson, Wilbert, 44, 52
Robison, Frank, 3, 30
Robison Park, 80
Rochester, NY, 60
Roettger, Walley, 60
Roggin, Joe, 69
Roosevelt, President Franklin D., 68, 113
Roosevelt Stadium, 113
"Rooters Row", 11
Rose Bowl, 118
Rose, H.M., 24
Rosen, Al, 104, 106
Rosen, Goodie, 72
Roush, Edd, 75
Roush, Eddie, 49
Rowe, Schoolboy, 68
Ruffing, Red, 97
Ruppert, Colonel Jacob, 39, 86
Ruppert, Jake, 56
Ruth, Babe, 16, 30, 31, 39, 55, 56, 57, 59, 63, 65, 67, 77, 85, 94, 105

S

Sain, Johnny, 89, 103, 115
Sallee, Harry "Slim", 49
Samuel H. French & Co., 27
San Diego, CA, 66
San Francisco, 63, 117
San Francisco Giants, 71
San Francisco Seals, 66
Sandy Springs, Maryland, 55
Schalk, Ray, 54
Schang, Wally, 39
Schenley Park, 24
Schmeling, Max, 61
"Schnozz", 75
Schreckengost ("Schreck"), Ossee, 9
Schriver, William, 46
Schulte, Frank, 19
Schumacher, Hal, 65
"Scooter", 96
Seals Stadium, 117
Seventh Regiment Band, 56
Sheckard, Jimmy, 19
Shibe, Ben, 2, 22
Shibe Park, 22, 24, 27, 30, 31, 32, 36, 47, 61, 87, 109
Simmons, Al, 61, 65
Simmons, Curt, 94
Sinclair, Harry, 44
Sisler, George, 77
Slagle, Jimmy, 19
Slaughter, Enos "Country", 82, 85, 110, 112
"Slick", 101
Smith, Earl, 58
Snider, Duke, 122
Sousa, John Phillip, 56
South End Grounds, 30
Southern Pines, N.C., 43
Southworth, Billy, 60
"Spahn and Sain and Pray for Rain", 89
Spahn, Warren, 89, 115
Spalding, Albert Goodwill, 26
Speaker, Tris, 37, 77
Spiders, 8 (Also see National League Spiders)
Sportsman's Park, 59, 67, 80, 82, 85
Springfield, MA, 53
St. Louis, 43, 59, 71, 104
St. Louis Browns, 3, 33, 43, 54, 59, 65, 67, 80, 92, 105, 109
St. Louis Cardinals, 17, 46, 59, 60, 65, 75, 79, 80, 85, 99, 101, 112
St. Louis Gashouse Gang, 69
Stahl, Jake, 39
Standard Network, 90

Steinfeld, Harry, 10
Stephens, Vern "Junior", 82, 92
Stephenson, Riggs, 60
Stoneham, Horace, 117
"Stonewall Infield", 19
Stovall, George, 43
Street, Gabby, 46
Stribling, Young, 61
Strikeout Story, 88
Strub, Dr. Charles, 117
Summers, Ed, 28
Sunday, Reverend Billy, 47
"Superchief", 102

T

Taft, President William Howard, 27, 35, 96
Taylor, Dummy, 7, 9
Taylor, Frank H., 23
"Teddy Ballgame", 78
Temple, Col. William, 3
Temple Cup, 3, 7
Terrapin Park, 43, 44
Terry, Bill, 65, 71
"The $11,000 Beauty", 40
"The $11,000 Lemon", 40
"The Baseball Palace of the World", 30
"The Big Cat", 101
"The Big Three", 107
"The Boy Manager", 57
"The Centerfielder's Riding the Red Wing", 90
The Diamond, 52
"The Giants Mealticket", 65
"The Hitless Wonders", 11
"The House That Ruth Built", 56
"The Kid", 78
"The Little Napolean", 29
"The Little Professor", 81
"The Splendid Splinter", 78
"The Thumper", 78
"There's a bit of little boy in every good ballplayer, 116
Thomson, Bobby, 83
Three Rivers Stadium, 6
Thurston, Sloppy, 59
Tiger Stadium, 3, 32
Tigers, 3, 19, 28, 68, 77, 79
Tinker, Joe, 10, 15, 20, 43
"Tip Tops", 22
Toledo of the American Association, 87
Topping, Dan, 86
Townball, 74
Trans Canada Airlines, 103
Traynor, Pie, 58

Tri-State League, 24
Tribe, 102, 107
Truman, President Harry S., 109
Turley, Bob, 104

U

Umpires, 97
Uncle David Beasley's Farm, 20
"Uncle Robbie", 52
Unglaub, Robert Alexander "Bob", 28
University of California, 13
University of Cincinnati, 122
University of Illinois, 60

V

Valo, Elmer, 110
Van Meter, Iowa, 88
Van Patrick, 88
Veeck, Bill, 62, 89, 104
Veterans Stadium, 27, 109
"Voice of the Detroit Tigers", 97
"Voice of the Red Sox", 100

W

Waddell, Rube, 9
Wagner, Honus, 1, 7, 17, 22, 40, 77
Wahoo Nebraska, 17
"Wahoo Sam", 17
Waldorf Astoria Hotel, 6
Walker, Gee, 68
Walker, Harry, 85
Walker, Moses Fleetwood, 87
Walker, Welday, 87
Walsh, "Big Ed", 11, 13
Walsh, Mike, 93
Walters, Bucky, 73, 76
Ward, Arch, 65
Ward, George, 22
Ward, Robert, 22
Warneke, Lon, 63, 65
Washington, 4, 39, 62
Washington Monument, 46, 83
Washington Park, 22
Washington Post, 35
Washington Senators, 2, 28, 34, 38, 46, 55, 57, 58, 65, 66, 71, 86, 96, 108, 111
Washington University, 19
WBZ, 53
Weaver, Buck, 48
Webb, Del, 86
"Wee-Ah", 12
Weeghman, John, 43

Weeghman Park (Wrigley Field), 30, 43, 60
Welker, Senator Herman, 111
Wertz, Vic, 118
West Side Park, 19, 20, 21, 27
West, Stan, 65
Westinghouse Engineers, 53
Whales, 43
Wheat, Zach, 52
White, Doc, 11
White Elephants, 27
White Engineering Company, 56
White House, 68
White Sox, 119 (Also see Chicago White Sox)
White Stockings, 47
"Whiz Kids", 109
Wilkerson, Thaddeus, 4, 5
Willett, Ed, 28
Williams, Claude "Lefty", 48
Williams, Ken, 54
Williams, Ted, 66, 78, 121
Wilson, Hack, 59
Wilson, Jimmie, 65
Windsor, Ontario, 103
Wise, Arthur C., 45
WJZ, 53
WMCA, 97
Wood, Smokey Joe, 39

Wooster, Massachusetts, 59
World War II, 67, 78, 79, 80, 82, 87, 88, 106
Worlds Fair, 65 (Also see Century of Progress)
Wright, George, 24
Wrigley Family, 79
Wrigley Field, 43, 79, 81, 118, 122 (Also see
   Weeghman Park)
Wrigley, William, 60
Wynn, Early, 107, 108
Wyse, Hank, 81

Y

Yankee Stadium, 38, 45, 56, 57, 59, 63, 79, 83, 86,
   95, 102, 121
Yankees, 10, 39, 44, 53, 54, 57, 58, 60, 61, 63, 65,
   66, 67, 71, 73, 79, 94, 96, 106, 116, 119, 120 , 121,
   122 (Also see New York Yankees)
Yawkee, Tom, 66, 92
Yawkee, William, 37
Yde, Emil, 58
Young, Cy, 3, 6, 77, 115 (Also see Cy Young Award)
Young, Denton True, 24

Z

Zarilla, Al, 82
Zernial, Gus, 98, 110
Zimmerman, Heinie, 40